AF679602

# Eigenstate Ciphernetic Techneme and Infoveining

Yafeh Visio

Eigenstate Ciphernetic Techneme and Infoveining

First Edition December 2025



Written by Yafeh Visio

# TABLE OF CONTENTS

# CHAPTER 1

# INTRODUCTION

## INTRODUCTION

Nowadays, secure communication is essential in the network field, mainly wireless communication. Security is a primary need for the organization (Rahul Aggarwal *et al.* 2011) and the entire developer to secure the document (NurAtiqah Muhammad *et al.* 2011). Cryptography is used widely in social networks and open environments to maintain the records securely, but some hackers still easily break the firewall and capture the data (Muhammad Mubashir Khan *et al.* 2010). In Mobile Ad hoc Network (MANET), cryptography is an emerging field that focuses on application-oriented like in military operations; legitimate users share the confidential information which the hacker hijacked due to malicious nodes (Anju Chahal *et al.* 2014). The original message is encrypted to broadcast the data in the network using the pair-wise key. Once the data is transmitted, the receiver node needs to identify the correct key to decrypt the message; otherwise, a node will stamp as a malicious node (Rahul Aggarwal *et al.* 2011, Mohamed Elboukhari *et al.* 2010).

Broadcasting, communication infrastructure, and digital transactions such as the web, e-mail, and mobile phones use encryption (Mohamed Elboukhari *et al.* 2010). Most traditional cryptographic algorithms are linked to particular mathematical operations and involve complex numerical strategies to prevent eavesdropping from discovering the information of encoded transmissions (Rishi Dutt Sharma 2011). Nevertheless, it has been found that this type of security may be susceptible to quantum computation's great capacity (Fei Gao *et al.* 2010), and thus conservative cryptographic cannot ensure key protection (Rishi Dutt Sharma 2011).

### Network Security

Network security is most commonly used to protect raw information in the communication area. It consists of policies and procedures to avoid and track the unauthorized access, abuse, alteration, or denial of connectivity of nodes in the network. An authority manages the node with permission to share or acquire data via the internet. The user needs a username and password or other authentication knowledge to access the network communication. Network security encompasses several jobs that are handled day by day in public and private sectors like the bank, business-government agencies, companies, organizations, etc.; the security is not only to protect the document and network resource by providing a unique key or password to the corresponding username.

### Security Management

The Security management differs from MANET or Wireless Sensor Network (WSN). For example, a home or small organization needs minimum security maintenance only, but in a large organization, the security needs high care to increase the weakness of malicious attacks from external threats to the network and improve the security verifications.

The MANET designs to transmit the data from an unmanned area in wireless mode. The IEEE802.11 standards are used in the device, introduced in 1997 with different frequencies from 2.4 - to 5GZH, and this type of sensor consumes more energy for transmitting data. So the research community developed a new protocol for reducing energy consumption and improving the authenticated transaction called IEEE 802.11.5.4. MANET security is the most trending technology these days. Day by day, the MANET security involvement increases, so the research community developed the MANET security to the next level. There are two varieties of attacks are in malicious nodes:

- Passive Attack
- Active Attack

The Ad hoc network is classified into some types:

Ad hoc networks are beneficial in natural catastrophes, army rescue missions, or just transferring connections between different personal computers because of their self-supporting architecture. However, there are infrastructural and performance limitations to an ad hoc network in the real universe, despite its user-friendliness and adaptability. The different kinds of wireless ad hoc communication:

**MANETs (Mobile Ad hoc Networks):** A MANET is a wirelessly connected self-forming network of mobile devices.

**VANETs (Vehicular ad hoc networks):** All nodes are installed with camera and microphones to monitor the movement of the animal in the forest. It needs high energy, bandwidth and QoS etc.

**SPANs (Smartphone ad hoc networks):** The SPAN is a commercial cellular network which is to establish peer-to-peer connectivity amongst terminals that can travel in any location to keep an eye on the surrounding region.

**WMN (Wireless Mesh Networks):** These are channels of radio wave nodes that use a mesh architecture to communicate. Tablets, cellphones, and other wireless devices are commonly used as users on networks.

**WSNs (Wireless Sensor Networks):** The terminals monitor the physical world for things like noise, pressure, and weather patterns. WSNs are utilized in various applications, including traffic management, vehicular identification, and greenhouses surveillance.

## MOTIVATION

The terminals in a MANET are self-configured, having resource-constrained capabilities, including bandwidth, energy backup, and processing capacity. However, due to the continuously changing architecture, lack of infrastructure, and susceptibility of routes and endpoints, secure data transfer is a critical responsibility in MANET. In this case, the exchange of packet from one node to another have less security and more packet loss occurs. In this scenario, the new algorithm is introduced to reduce the packet loss and improve the authentication process called QECC.

In QECC algorithm, the nodes are divided into two parts weakest node and strongest node. By using this algorithm the un-trusted nodes are automatically eliminate from the route and it provides the best trusted route from this another proposed protocol is introduced called PREVENT. The protocol used to find the trusted path to transmit the data by using frequent pattern mining technique which used to mine knowledge from the node to spot the misbehaviors node time to time. Confidentiality, node coordination, isolation, and privacy should be necessary for protection. Sharing images with pals needs less protection than sharing essential data with company executives.

Furthermore, not all endpoints may be capable of running routes and security measures. For whatever type of equipment and circumstance, power restrictions, node variation, failure rate, and limited bandwidth need the formulation and construction of flexible route and protection methods. It's tricky to handle complex patterns with variable identities, group signings, and dispersed electronic signatures (Zhang *et al.* 2015). In wireless ad hoc networks, key agreement techniques for node permission and identity authentication are necessary to accomplish seamless connectivity and node permission.

The network node's dynamic implementation intellects packets from the source to the forwarder/destination node without any collision and modification. In the dynamic topology the retransmission and node failure also occurs. The MANET need to establish a best and secure path for transmission of good quality of packets, reduce error rate improve the trust level between the nodes and loss of packets. The main advantage of the MANET in cryptography is

- We must protect Communication among nodes from attacks on secrecy, but no appropriate access management or permission control procedures are recommended. It should neutralize the DoS attack in this system to guarantee the network's node's stability.

- From the perspective of service supply, the spread of responsibilities and obligations considerably decreases the risks that would emerge in the infrastructure if we use centralized techniques.

- The facilities and services are crucial in commercial solutions since the infrastructure may have to scale quickly, and the service provider's trustworthiness depends on the channel's and services' serviceability.

In the MANET, the communication of the node can be formed in together or separated on the operation management. The development of a routing algorithm is quite challenging to imply the authenticated transmissions of data in dynamic network topology, due to infrastructure-less communication. Meanwhile, the key management also playing a vital role in the MANET to provide the best result for the network security in various services like trust model, cryptosystem, key establishment, key storage, and key sharing.

The use of traditional cryptographic methods such as AES 256-bit encryption can indeed provide strong security protection in many applications. However, there are some limitations of these methods when applied to MANETs.

One of the main limitations is the dynamic nature of MANETs, where nodes may join or leave the network at any time. This poses a challenge for traditional cryptographic methods, as the distribution of keys and management of secure channels between nodes becomes difficult and complex. Additionally, MANETs are vulnerable to various types of attacks, including eavesdropping, impersonation, and denial of service attacks, which can compromise the security of the network.

Quantum computing approaches, such as Quantum Cryptography and Quantum Elliptic Curve Cryptography (QECC), can potentially overcome these limitations by leveraging the principles of quantum mechanics. These approaches can provide unique advantages, such as secure key distribution and authentication, resistance to certain types of attacks, and the ability to detect any eavesdropping attempts. These advantages can significantly enhance the security of MANETs.

Therefore, the adoption of quantum computing approaches can provide a more secure solution for MANETs, especially in scenarios where traditional cryptographic methods may not be sufficient. This motivation highlights the need for exploring new cryptographic approaches, and quantum computing provides a promising avenue for addressing the security challenges in MANETs.

The study and motivation of the work is to design a new protocol for finding the trusted path and to reduce the vulnerability node in the network. The main issue is the layer structure does not supports the valid encryption mechanism in the node. So, it needs to improve the performance level and trust level for authenticated transmission and to reduce the error rate also to improve the throughput.

The non-cryptographic method of identifying malicious MANET nodes, such as the data path mining approach with combinatorial methods, has a different motivation compared to cryptographic methods like QECC and ECC.

One of the main motivations behind using non-cryptographic methods is that they can be more efficient and scalable compared to cryptographic methods. Cryptographic methods like QECC and ECC require complex mathematical operations, and the use of quantum computing in QECC can further increase the computational resources needed. In contrast, non-cryptographic methods can be based on more straightforward data analysis techniques, which can be easier to implement and optimize.

Another motivation for using non-cryptographic methods is that they can be used to complement cryptographic methods. While cryptographic methods can provide strong security guarantees, they may not be able to detect certain types of attacks or malicious behaviors. Non-cryptographic methods, on the other hand, can be used to analyze network traffic and identify anomalous patterns or behaviors that may indicate malicious nodes. By combining both cryptographic and non-cryptographic methods, a more comprehensive and robust security framework can be established for MANETs.

Overall, the choice of using either cryptographic or non-cryptographic methods for securing MANETs depends on the specific requirements and constraints of the network. While cryptographic methods like QECC and ECC can provide strong security guarantees, non-cryptographic methods can offer more efficiency and scalability, as well as complement the limitations of cryptographic methods.

## ALLEGATION OF PROBLEMS IN MOBILE AD HOC NETWORK

In several routing protocol are existing only for the route optimization and to found the optimal path. In MANET, the many protocols define only for the secure packet transmission in particular region and area. The existing protocols discard the packet or node which is delayed are not responding properly in the network. So, in this thesis it examines the accuracy and metrics of the trusted routes are established.

In MANET, the research are actively representing the security problems occurs in between the nodes and also in network areas. The node are self-configured and autonomous communicating characteristics of MANET. There are many wireless medium are designed with limited battery power, dynamic network topology and propagation delay due to security issue. Some security are not possible to use in MANET which are presently successful in wired network. The various problems occurs in MANET are follows:

- Active snooping and passively tampering make MANETs more vulnerable to assaults.

- It is exceedingly challenging to deploy the protection mechanisms due to the lack of Relying on third-party add-ons.
- Smartphones are impotent against DoS attacks due to their limited energy consumption and compute capabilities, as they are unable to execute security mechanisms that need heavy calculations, such as public-key cryptosystems.
- Because MANETs are infrastructure-free and self-configuring, trustworthy stations have more opportunities to be exploited and launch network attacks.
- Because of the node transportation system, distinguishing between stale and faked forwarding data is complex. It allows repeated network reconfiguring in the node movement process, which increases the danger of assaults.

The MANET has some of nodes are changed based on the congestion/collision of data due to following attacks:

- Route sequence numbers modification
- Hop Count modification attack
- Source route modification attack
- Wormhole attack
- Black hole attack

## OBJECTIVES

The main objectives of the research work are

- To learn and build up the malicious attack model and test with the QKD protocol with proposed security algorithm called Quantum Elliptic Curve Cryptography (QECC) algorithm to find the fool around node that is weakest node and brawny (strongest) node in the network to improve the trust level in MANET.

- To analyze the security performance with the existing Algorithm for Adhoc Wireless Secure Communication (AWSC) and the proposed Quantum Elliptic Curve Cryptography (QECC) and Prevention and Eviction of Vulnerable Enemy Nodes in Trusted (PREVENT) network is used to from cluster between two part of node called weak node and good node which easy to find the best and secure path for transmission.

- To examine the performance of multi-path communication with various parameter such as throughput, energy, packet loss and trust level.

## RESEARCH METHODOLOGY

Quantum key exchange is a relatively new notion in quantum computation, which needs to classify the secret key sharing mechanism in between the nodes. In this research work, the techniques have been used to solve the various attack which is present in the cryptographic like resend and empirical attack. The research work is proposed in some phases:

- According to the QECC first it calculates the number of pairwise keys need for a network. Based on that the key is shared with the node by using cryptography technique. The QECC is using asymmetric key cryptographic method to distribute key to each node with their ID number which is compute by hash function.

- In second phase, the node to node communication will occurs here the quantum key distribution algorithm is used to calculate the number of pairwise key generation time and the number packet transferred from node to node is calculated to identify the fool node and strong node.

- Calculate the error rate of each node to deduct and remove from the path. Based on the packet size the node is have more than the threshold value automatically it eliminates from the routing path. This method is used for trust path selection and to find the fool around node and brawny node in the network.

- The last phase about the selection of trusted path by using the Data Path Combinatorial Approximation (DPCA) algorithm. The path-set is generation of path from the set of paths on any node which are provided paths to various other nodes participating in the data transmission. The mining algorithm is based on Approximate Inclusion-Exclusion technique. Without continual path scanning, approximate counts are calculated for the path-sets

- The proposed techniques are used in Network Simulator - 2 (NS2) to examine and analyze the performance of the multi-path communication with various parameter such as throughput, energy, packet loss and trust level.

## SCOPE OF RESEARCH

This study aims to boost node trustworthiness by finding the fool around node (misbehaving) nodes at different percentile levels existing in MANETs. The table below represents what people like. To use the QECC and DPCA algorithms, the First algorithm, QECC, uses quantum bits to generate keys among nodes; each node validates the neighbor key before every transaction. If the node fails to share the key or any failure in authentication will lead the node to be delisted. The delisted nodes are clustered and form the malicious group, and we can separate the hostile group from the good active nodes. Also, with the help of DPCA, you'll need a path table and a prevalent node-set table. The entire transaction of nodes is stored in the path-set database. The typical node-set table comprises node metadata for which nodes that engage in transactions regularly are recognized and clustered together. This database contains the minimum support each node provides to its neighbors based on every successful process. As more transactions are completed successfully, the node's support count will increase. The node-set is detected and recorded for the forthcoming network activity.

The trust path and error rate are verifies that the parameters are improves the throughput. The route establishment between nodes is ensured increasing in reliability and reduce malicious node.

## SIGNIFICANCE OF RESEARCH WORK

The target to do this research work is to carry out the quantum key distribution function to fulfill the selection of trusted path to improve the quality of network, path found and less energy consumption in the dynamic topology in MANET. The performance of the suggested algorithm to attain the various secure communications between the nodes in network. In many aspects the parameter are compared with the existing protocols and algorithms which improved and additional reduction of the energy consumptions and key generation time.

## ORGANIZATION OF THE THESIS

The thesis comprises of seven chapter with the detail of the study carried out to the performance of the various data packet are compared and the throughput were calculated to attain the maximum results for the following parameters such as power consumption, packet delivery rate, and node-to-node delay. Some of the literature cited for the research topic is given in the reference.

**Chapter 1** deals with general introduction about the networks security, types of attack in MANET, motivations, objectives, importance of research work and scope of the present work.

**Chapter 2** describes the fundamentals of the Mobile Ad hoc Networks with block diagram, architecture, applications, design challenges and Security mechanisms & algorithms.

**Chapter 3** deals with the brief explanation about the various research work which are important to this thesis work.

**Chapter 4** describes about the suggested work of the "Quantum cryptography based on QECC". The simulation outcomes depicts that improving the throughput, energy, trust level and decreasing of packet loss when compare with various security mechanism

**Chapter 5** deals with the second proposed protocol called PREVENT, which shows the best and secured trusted path in the network. This chapter describes about the eviction of vulnerable node from the route.

**Chapter 6** describes the performance evaluation analysis and simulation result shows the outcomes of Quantum Elliptic Curve Cryptography (QECC) and PREVENT. The parameter assessments contrast several quantum key mechanisms that are already in use. Finally, we evaluate the suggested algorithm's performance for total calculation time and failure rate.

**Chapter 7** summaries the conclusion comments and potential improvements of the proposed methodologies are presented.

.

# CHAPTER 2

# WIRELESS MOBILE AD HOC NETWORKS IN SECURITY

## INTRODUCTION TO WIRELESS AD HOC NETWORKS

Ad hoc Network is an emerging field in wireless networks, which envisions applications ranging from military applications to sampling of statistical data. A group of independent devices are connected with each other in the presence of no physical mediums or taxonomy as shown in Figure 2.1. This model of usage and grouping nodes for a specific purpose was introduced by Charles Perkins *et al.* (2001). By the term independence, nodes/devices possess complete liberty to join and walk away from the other devices of the networks in a distributed order. One device may take lead and be deputed as routing node, which is made responsible for collecting data packets and forwarding them too their destined nodes. It assists the transmission by becoming an internal hop. The same node may initiate the data transfer and any other node may play the same role. Hence this Ad hoc networks are termed to be a free and infrastructure-less networks.

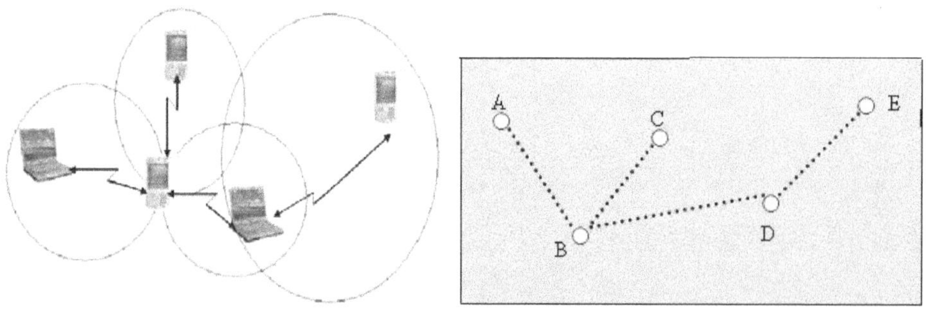


**Figure 2.1 Mobile Ad hoc Networks**

There is no central medium to regulate the process of data of transfer, to depute internal hops or to define the pathway between source device and destination device. The same measure of Ad hoc networks has a counter effect by forming unbroken links. Due to the fact that devices/nodes are dynamic in nature, unavailability of nodes for producing links and intern hops cannot be guaranteed. The issue is easily addressed in an automated fashion by enforcing a re-configuration by the devices themselves.

This function promises utmost connectivity between devices as they are self-configurable during failures. MANETS are further categorized into Static Ad hoc Networks (SANET) and Dynamic Ad hoc Networks (DANETS).

**MOBILE AD HOC NETWORKS**

Multiple devices that are capable of configuring their location and routing on their own are composed within architecture less network configuration. A common wireless medium is shared among the devices for communication purpose. This channel operates as a common mode of transferring packets to other participating nodes of the same network. The infrastructure and network hierarchy is represented in Figure 2.2 proposed that MANETs can be a suitable network for connecting mobile devices and establish a platform for efficiency and reliable communications.

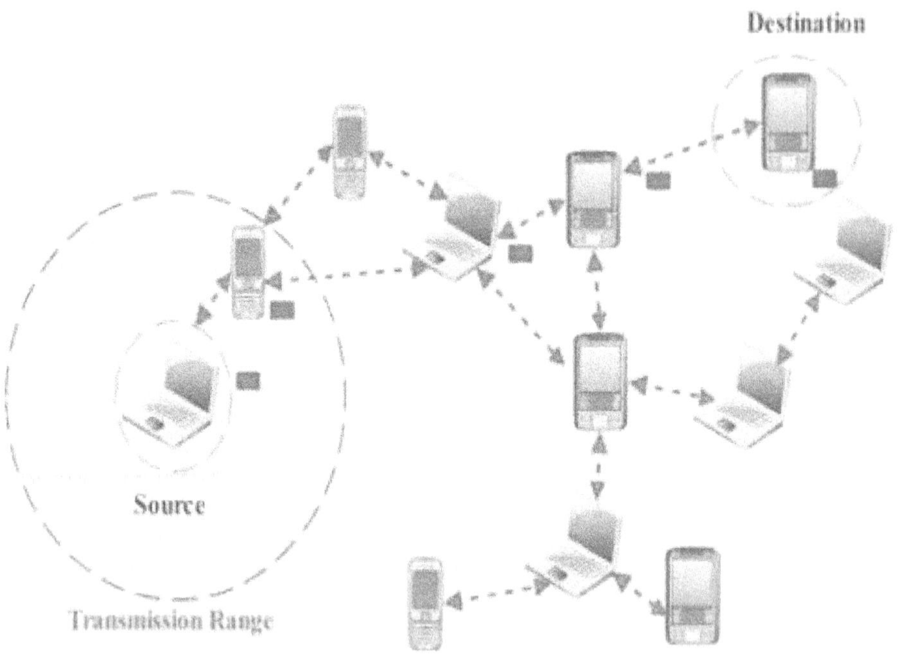


**Figure 2.2 Network Architecture and Transmission Range**

Nevertheless, mobile devices participating in the communication are restricted by various bounds such as energy of each node, bandwidth used for communication, range of transmission (mostly short ranges and minimal frequency).Though these factors are considered to be a controllable environment, the dynamic nature of mobile devices makes it difficult to define a clear routing protocol for such environment. Kui Wu *et al.* (2002) listed out the practical difficulties of predicting a routing protocol; in the presence of a multipath transmission paths existing between participating nodes. These networks also do not mandatorily require a Base Station. Baburaj *et al.* (2008) also proposed that routing becomes hectic since every node becomes a router when necessary. The complexity level in deriving an efficient routing protocol is increased when compared to that of Wireless Local Area Networks, where an access point streamlines the packet transfers and delivery.

## Issues in Design and Implementation of MANET

All mobile nodes can act as a source of packets, destination or router at any given time of execution. Given that the nodes can also act as router and intermediate hop, defining an efficient routing protocol has been a challenge in the recent past. Some of the standard issues are listed and explained in this section.

**Distributed Taxonomy:** Giuseppe Bianchi *et al.* (2002) described the MANET as a network without any fixed architecture or infrastructure and be distributed at the same time. In any distributed networks, there will not be any server that serves the multiple clients such as a peer to peer network. Having multiple nodes which require service from the Base Station at any given time, the mobile nodes are authenticated with minimal interventions, to increase the user-friendly experience to new users. At any given point of time, the services required by nodes are high and concurrent. Expectation of a Base Station will be to deliver services to its fullest potential. This criterion increases the burden of a sink node and without authentication or minimal authentication, an open network of devices is highly prone to attacks.

**Dynamic in Nature:** The authors Siva Ram Murthy *et al.* (2007), Wenqing *et al.* (2011) documented the capability of mobile nodes of self-organizing within the network. At any given time, there is no consistency in the position of nodes realizing that all nodes keep changing their location based on necessity. There is no prescribed or centralized server to regulate the inflow and outflow of message packets. Elasticity of a MANET, being its greatest strength, also increases the overhead of maintaining the nodes' locations and continued service whenever required.

**Energy limitations:** All nodes primarily run on in-built batteries with limited power and usually be deployed in remote and hostile environments. The power capacity of each node is completely limited and conserved at all times. Kui Wu *et al.* (2002) added multiple power conserving algorithms that mandates optimal usage of energy for every operation associated with it. All nodes are bound by a battery backup which restricts the nodes from prolonged usages. Being in a route for forwarding the nodes, be it the cluster heads, or even the source and destination nodes have limited energy and will continue to function until the battery power is available. Stationary nodes, typically the Base Station is powered by a durable source.

**Addressing Within the Topology:** A dynamic network will demand a quicker and ubiquitous addressing process in order to provide unique addresses to every node. Mobile Internet Protocol is employed in cellular networks in which the addresses of the modes are assigned by the Base Station. The same practice is not applicable in a MANET due to its dynamic nature. Chun Hung Richard *et al.* (2005) proposed a successful technique called Duplicate Address Resolution (DAR) to prevent the delay in addressing and assigning addresses to nodes like the base station would do.

**Size of the Network:** The application of MANET are limitless ranging from SMART and Virtual class rooms, networking within a large premise and providing service to multiple and independent devices. Many virtual boundaries and a physical connection were eliminated. Yet delay in background protocols limited the applicability of devices with an upper bound of network devices that can be connected to the current network.

**Properties of Mobile Ad hoc Networks**

**Wireless:** No physical connections are established within the networks devices and only the air is used as the medium to connect all participants.

**Adhoc:** The name denotes "for a purpose". All the nodes are unique, independent and self-catering to the requirements. No central server controls or commands the other nodes within the networks. All devices communicate through other nodes and may act as an intermediate hop if required.

**Multi-hop:** When a path has to be setup between source and destination nodes, the other participants form a path for the required transfer and clears the path, frees the devices for other path set ups. The nodes are capable of independent functioning even when they are blocked within a set up path, resulting in generation of impartial information.

**Dynamic:** No node possesses a constant position within the network and may travel at different speeds to change the topology in a high variation environment. The architecture randomly changes its structure any time.

**Limitation of Energy and Bandwidth:** Vital energy utilization is mandatory for devices with inbuilt and limited power resources. The energy efficiency also guarantees the performance of the entire network. Similarly, the frequency and bandwidth of the medium has to be put into proper utilization. Wastage of energy and bandwidth will lead to wastage of resources, resulting in dead nodes and unreliable communication between devices.

### 2.5.3 Applications of MANET

MANETs are implemented in a wide range of applications from a class room to a battleground

1. Tactical Environment
2. Rescue Operations
3. Real Time Communication
4. Educational Services
5. Medical Assistance
6. Disaster Management

**MANET Quality of Service**

Technological advancements have made the MANETs cheaper to implement and easier to be deployed in area where there is limited or near zero possibilities of establishing physical network. The years have evolved from usage of phones wired to digital satellite broadcasting. Apart from the challenges discussed like routing and energy management, ensuring quality is also an important expectation of MANETs especially while transferring tent video/audio files and images.

Qualities of Service factors rely on the parameters which are affected during transfer of information from a start node to end node. Throughput being low, number of lost and dropped packets, errors in transmission, latency, out of order connections and delivery, jitter are some of the QoS parameters. These issues have to be addressed before a reliable communication network id designed and implemented. Network behavior of a MANET will be dependent on efficient monitoring of nodes, maintenance of routes and ensuring stability. Node to Node delay of message packets from start to end has to be reduced, lowering the energy consumption of every node and without increasing the control overhead.

## SECURITY IN MANET

Protection has become a top priority to offer shielded communication between multiple nodes in a dangerous environment. However, unlike wired networks, the distinctive properties of MANETs provide a variety of nontrivial design and implementation issues, such as unsecured peer-to-peer network technology, shareable wireless channel, restrictive resource limitations, and fast-changing network structure. These issues demonstrate the need for multi-fence security mechanisms that provide broad protection and proper network management. The essential security concern of preserving the multi-hop communication link among wireless nodes in a MANET is the topic of this paper. We analyze the security difficulties that this situation raises, explore the complexities of security architecture, and examine the most up-to-date security recommendations for MANET link- and network management of transmitting packets across multi-hop wireless channels. The comprehensive security strategy must cover both tiers and include all three security mechanisms: preventive, surveillance, and response.

A MANET is a collection of mobile or wireless devices connected without the need for any architecture. The system is self-organizing and adapts to variations in topology caused by movement or connection disruptions. The transmitters on the collaborating network elements have a restricted channel for communication. Nodes pass messages for other nodes to communicate with nodes beyond their straight wireless connectivity radius, leading to multi-hop pathways. As MANETs move closer to widespread adoption, security concerns have grown important. If ad-hoc networking is unsafe, we cannot use it in practice. For instance, in situations like disaster rescue and combat transmission, an enemy can effectively prevent network construction since no security protocol is used. Throughout the last century, obtaining safety for electronic voice, sound, and visual communications has been a significant concern. The complexity of this task arises from the belief that such a type of transport is highly susceptible to delays. As a result, it's critical to use an effective and easy way to safeguard this type of information when sending it through ad-hoc connections.

Almost every study of protection in Ad-Hoc networks has found that the authentication process is too complicated or the defense is inadequate. Moreover, because audio data transfer over Ad-Hoc networks is challenging to manage, few academics have focused on it. Kerberos is the most widely used dispersed authentication service in ad-hoc networking, and it allows a client to authenticate its identification to servers without trying to send data through the network. However, the scheme's fundamental flaw was ineffective against key guessing assaults. The poor infrastructure in MANETs also precludes the adoption of server-based mechanisms like Kerberos. A certification is disseminated using a threshold secret sharing technique in certificate-based approaches. Each entity owns a small piece of the pie, and numerous units (K) in a given neighborhood work together to supply the entire service. However, if specific insider threats (team members) are involved, this is a disaster. It also necessitates using a Trusted Third Party (TTP) to set up a community. i.e., a trustworthy dealer is used to obtain hidden shares.

A substantial percentage of predetermined and widely disclosed keys finds in various key management strategies for MANETs. Each node determines keys at irregular intervals and keeps track of the keys it shares with everyone. It keeps the data under wraps and generates a group key using the shared keys. It also makes it easier to establish secure ad-hoc networks widely. The disadvantage is that key dispersal in Ad-hoc systems adds to the overhead. Each node's encryption keys in Addressing Cryptographic

System-based techniques (ACS) are made up of a node addressing component, and a network-wide central component node-to-node verification is provided by ACS using the node addresses and certificate-less cryptographic. Only approved nodes are permitted to partake in each hop seen between sender and recipient. All authorized nodes are aware of the key formation process.

Data encryption of voice data with stream ciphering is a simple and effective method when we produce powerful and randomized keys, and streaming cipher will become more safe and reliable. FARA (Fast Anti Random Approximate) was suggested previously as a simple way of creating anti-random key sequences. Anti-random sequences have gained popularity, and it demonstrates to have more robust statistical parameters than pseudo-random integers, suggesting that we can use them for stream substitution cipher. We can pair it with Channel ciphering to improve security while keeping things simple. However, because of the massive data volume and significant duplication, conventional cryptographic techniques like DES and its counterpart work inadequately for multimedia information. We offer a system in which audio data transfers safely using a simple stream substitution cipher approach, but the key generates randomly using the FARA technique, rendering it more reliable. Furthermore, the sound information is encrypted and decoded at each node, and the password is rendered extra safe by encoding and decoding the key at every node to use the RSA technique, with the private and public credentials produced using node location-based cryptographic techniques.

**Key Exchanging Technique using RSA**

Exchanging keys using the RSA mechanism (Yong Yu *et al.* 2007). The RSA encryption scheme is the biggest and most popular public-key encryption technique. It uses encoded communication without requiring the exchanging of a private key. We can do both data encryption and digital certificates with the RSA technique. The complexity of factoring tremendous values is the basis for its protection. A node location-based cryptographic approach we use to provide information security. Only authorized nodes can participate in this since we use node addresses in the encryption and decrypting mechanism. All approved nodes will decode the key, add their data, verify the path, then decode it with their secret key. The next node decodes it using the shared key of the preceding node, and so on. It will render the key more private and have minimal time spent on this procedure.

**Security Challenges in MANET**

The most important challenges in the ad hoc networks are:

1. Availability
2. Integrity
3. Confidentiality
4. Authenticity
5. Non-Repudiation
6. Authorization
7. Anonymity
8. No Secure Boundaries
9. Power and Computational L imitations
10. Lack of Centralized Management Facility
11. Cooperativeness

### Characteristics of MANET

MANETs have the following key features:

1. Self-organization and management
2. The majority of the nodes are movable.
3. The network topology shifts.
4. Heterogeneous in nature
5. Infrastructure less
6. All node acts as a router and a host.
7. Routing with many hops
8. Limitation of power
9. Scale variation
10. Decentralize topology
11. Pathways of variable routing
12. Topology that is always changing
13. No need for an access point
14. Broadcasted Operation

### Security Mechanisms over MANET

Intrusion detection and secure route technologies are MANET's main types of security approaches. The attacker node intercepts all packets and saves them for later use. In this article, we'll go over security in-depth-the detailed information on the security requirements of MANET in Figure 2.3.

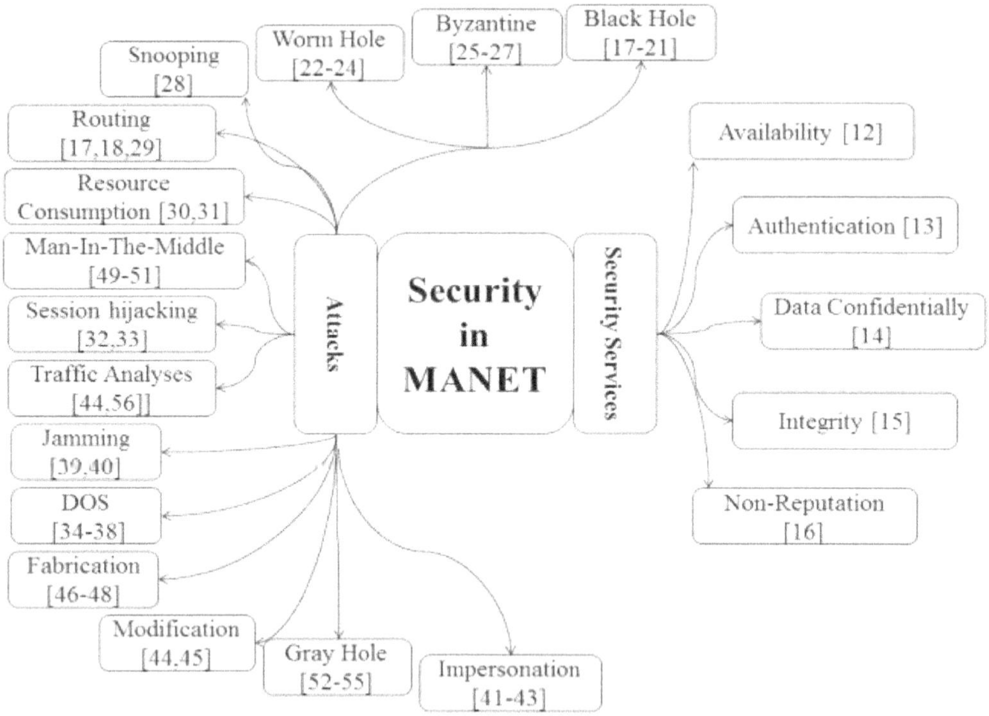


**Figure 2.3 Security Aspects in MANET**

**Detect the presence of Intruders:** An Intrusion Prevention System (IPS) is a critical component of any network security. Its primary purpose is to discover suspected security policy breaches by continuously monitoring activity and reacting to those that appear to be intrusive. If we detect an intrusion in the networking, it launches a reaction to prevent or limit the system's harm.

**Misuse-Based Intrusion Detection:** Attack Detection Depending on Misuse, Detecting attacking signatures by Misuse-Based detection given the current system actions. Business IDSs often favor them because they are effective and have good accuracy. However, the most significant disadvantage is that it is incapable of detecting fresh attacks. In addition, because the system is only as robust as its signature repository, periodic data updates are required.

**Intrusion detection depending on anomalies:** Detects intrusions as anomalies or variations from usual behavioral patterns. The likelihood of regular activity we recognize as abnormalities by IDS is high with anomaly-based identification, and it can identify undiscovered threats.

**Anomaly Detection Based on Specifications:** In this section, intruders are discovered as real-time violations of routing protocol requirements. They're commonly used to identify forging and alteration assaults. On the other hand, this approach is unable to detect assaults that do not explicitly break protocol standards.

## SUMMARY

This chapter discussed about the architecture of MANET, block diagram of MANET security challenges of MANET, distinctiveness of ad hoc networks and classification of MANET. The MANET which as lot demand in the research world which focused to examine and solve the problem in the energy efficiency, finding of trusted path and error rate.

# CHAPTER 3

# LITERATURE SURVEY

## QUANTUM CRYPTOGRAPHIC MECHANISM

We can break down Traditional cryptography's primary flaws into three categories. First, attackers could use the prevalence of some algorithmic weaknesses to compromise the system's protection. The following fundamental issue with cryptographic techniques is the computation of low life expectancy. As a result, in goal is to expand the life expectancy period; an increase in the key length is a must.

Finally, conventional cryptographic techniques demand a greater quantity of processing to be efficient. Change to quantum computation to get around this. Quantum Secret Share (QSS), Quantum Key Distribution (QKD), Quantum Identity Authentication (QIA), and Quantum Protected Straight Transmission are some of the most common uses of cryptographic algorithms. Table 3.1 summarizes current achievements in Quantum Computing.

**Table 3.1 Achievements in quantum computing**

| S. No. | Name of the Researchers and University | Title | Year | Achievements | Reference Website |
|---|---|---|---|---|---|
| 1 | Ann Arbor, University of Michigan | "U-M develops scalable and mass-producible quantum computer chip". | 2005 | Constructed a semiconductor device that operated as an ionic trap | http://ns.umich.edu/index.html?Releases/2005/Dec05/r121205b |
| 2 | DiCarlo, Chow, Gambetta, Lev S Bishop, Johnson, Schuster, Majer, Blais, Frunzio, Girvin, Schoelkopf, Yale University | "Demonstration of two-qubit algorithms with a superconducting quantum processor" | 2009 | The first primitive strong quantum processor was developed. Basic computations might be executed on the two-qubit super conductivity device. | https://www.nature.com/articles/nature08121 |
| 3 | University of Bristol | "Code-breaking quantum algorithm runs on a silicon chip". | 2010 | Classical and quantum optics, researchers developed a silicon-based quantum computer processor. Upon that chip, the researchers were able to perform Shor's technique. | www.newscientist.com/article/dn17736-codebreaking-quantum-algorithm-run-on-a-silicon-chip.html |
| 4 | Australian and Japan scientist | "Engadget, First light wave quantum teleportation achieved, opens door to ultra fast data transmission". | 2011 | **Quantum teleportation:** A group of Australian and Japanese scientists has successfully transported a complex network of quantum information in the form of lights. | https://www.engadget.com/2011-04-18-first-light-wave-quantum-teleportation-achieved-opens-door-to-u.html |

**Table 3.1 (Continued)**

| S. No. | Name of the Researchers and University | Title | Year | Achievements | Reference Website |
|---|---|---|---|---|---|
| 5 | D-wave systems | "Learning to program the D-Wave One" | 2011 | Announced the first commercial Quantum annealer. Also built 128 qubit processor chipset. | https://dwave.wordpress.com/2011/05/11/learning-to-program-the-d-wave-one/ |
| 6 | IBM scientist | "IBM Says It's 'On the Cusp' of Building a Quantum Computer" | 2012 | Manufactured superconducting qubits using proven micro-fabrication technologies employed for silicon technology, allowing the company to expand to thousands or even millions of quantum bits in the future. | https://www.pcmag.com/archive/ibm-says-its-on-the-cusp-of-building-a-quantum-computer-294785 |
| 7 | University of Southern California | Quantum computer built inside diamond | 2012 | A scientist group has created the first quantum computer in a diamond, with protections over "decoherence" – noise that inhibits the processor from working correctly. | https://www.sciencedaily.com/releases/2012/04/120404161943.htm |

**Table 3.1 (Continued)**

| S. No. | Name of the Researchers and University | Title | Year | Achievements | Reference Website |
|---|---|---|---|---|---|
| 8 | The Quantum Artificial Intelligence Lab (also called the Quantum AI Lab or QuAIL) is a joint initiative of NASA, Universities Space Research Association, and Google | "Launching the Quantum Artificial Intelligence Lab". | 2013 | Scientists are exploring more precise and effective models for everything from voice recognition to internet search to protein folding. | https://ai.googleblog.com/2013/05/launching-quantum-artificial.html |
| 9 | National Security Agency(NSA) | "NSA seeks to build quantum computer that could crack most types of encryption" | 2014 | The race to develop "a cryptological usable quantum computer" — a machine capable of breaking practically every type of encryption now used to safeguard financial, healthcare, commercial, and government documents all around the globe. | https://www.washingtonpost.com/world/national-security/nsa-seeks-to-build-quantum-computer-that-could-crack-most-types-of-encryption/2014/01/02/8fff297e-7195-11e3-8def-a33011492df2_story.html |

**Table 3.2 Comparison of the similarities and differences between his method and the existing ones and highlight the strengths/advantages of the proposed method over the existing ones.**

| Paper | Approach | QECC Similarities | QECC Differences | Advantages of QECC |
|---|---|---|---|---|
| My Research Paper | Proposed QECC method | Utilizes quantum computing to enhance elliptic curve cryptography for MANETs | Utilizes QKD to generate and transfer keys, and combines with ECC for authentication | Provides stronger security and authentication compared to traditional cryptographic methods; Provides faster and more efficient key generation and transfer compared to classical methods |
| "Quantum Key Distribution based on Correlated Probabilistic Polarization" (2021) by M. Darvish | Uses polarized photons for QKD | Both use QKD and ECC | Uses polarized photons instead of entangled photon pairs | QECC is more scalable and faster |
| "Secure Communication Protocol using Quantum Elliptic Curve Cryptography with Genetic Algorithm" (2021) by S. H. Mirjalili | Uses genetic algorithms to optimize key generation | Both use QKD and ECC | Uses genetic algorithms in key generation | QECC is more secure against quantum attacks |

**Table 3.2(Continued)**

| Paper | Approach | QECC Similarities | QECC Differences | Advantages of QECC |
|---|---|---|---|---|
| "Quantum Elliptic Curve Cryptography: A Review" (2022) by D. Makur et al. | Survey paper of various QECC methods | N/A | N/A | QECC is a promising area of research |
| "Quantum Public Key Cryptography Based on Elliptic Curve Cryptography" (2022) by Y. Cui et al. | Uses ECC for public key cryptography | Both use ECC | Uses a quantum approach for public key cryptography | QECC provides stronger security against quantum attacks |
| "QELIP: A Post-Quantum Signature Scheme Based on Elliptic Curve Cryptography and Quantum Key Distribution" (2022) by B. Ramkumar et al. | Combines QKD and ECC for signature schemes | Both use QKD and ECC | Uses a signature scheme approach | QECC is more versatile and can be used in various applications |
| "Qu ntum Cryptography Based on Quantum Elliptic Curve Cryptography and its Applications" (2021) by M. R. Mozaffari-Kermani et al. | Combines QKD and ECC for secure communication | Both use QKD and ECC | Uses a quantum approach for communication | QECC provides better security against quantum attacks and faster key exchange |

Table 3.2(Continued)

| Paper | Approach | QECC Similarities | QECC Differences | Advantages of QECC |
|---|---|---|---|---|
| "An Efficient Quantum Cryptographic System with ECC and QKD for WSN" (2021) by S. H. Park et al. | Uses ECC and QKD for secure communication in WSNs | Both use ECC and QKD | Uses a different method for QKD key generation | QECC provides more efficient and secure key generation |
| "A Quantum-Elliptic Curve Cryptography-Based Signcryption Scheme for the Internet of Things" (2022) by J. Zhang et al. | Uses QECC for secure communication in IoT | Both use QECC | Uses a signcryption scheme approach | QECC provides more efficient and versatile encryption and authentication |
| "QSMC: A Quantum Secret Sharing Scheme Based on Minkowski Sum with Elliptic Curve Cryptography" (2022) by T. Chen et al. | Uses Minkowski sum and ECC for quantum secret sharing | Both use ECC | Uses Minkowski sum method for secret sharing | QECC is more versatile and can be used in various applications |
| "Quantum elliptic curve cryptography: New trends and future prospects" (2022) by R. Kumar et al. | Survey paper of various QECC methods | N/A | N/A | QECC is a promising area of research |

**Table 3.2(Continued)**

| Paper | Approach | QECC Similarities | QECC Differences | Advantages of QECC |
|---|---|---|---|---|
| "Quantum Elliptic Curve Cryptography with Cloud Computing" (2023) by Y. Chen et al. | Uses cloud computing and ECC for quantum secure communication | Both use ECC | Uses cloud computing for key storage and management | QECC provides more efficient and secure key generation and transfer |
| "A Novel Quantum Cryptography Approach using Randomized Entangled Qubits" (2021) by M. B. Khan et al. | Uses randomized entangled qubits for QKD | Both use QKD and ECC | Uses randomized entangled qubits instead of traditional entangled qubits | QECC is more secure against attacks on entangled qubits |
| "Enhanced Quantum Cryptography Based on Elliptic Curve Cryptography and Chaotic Maps" (2021) by L. Wu et al. | Uses chaotic maps to enhance key generation | Both use QKD and ECC | Uses chaotic maps in key generation | QECC provides stronger security against attacks on key generation |
| "Quantum Elliptic Curve Cryptography Using Qubits in Nuclear Magnetic Resonance" (2022) by Y. Li et al. | Uses nuclear magnetic resonance to generate qubits | Both use QKD and ECC | Uses nuclear magnetic resonance to generate qubits | QECC is more scalable and less expensive than other quantum approaches |
| "A Quantum Key Distribution Scheme Using Shor's Algorithm for Elliptic Curve Cryptography" (2022) by X. Zhang et al. | Uses Shor's algorithm to break classical ECC | Both use QKD and ECC | Uses Shor's algorithm to break classical ECC | QECC is post-quantum and more secure against quantum attacks |

**Table 3.2(Continued)**

| Paper | Approach | QECC Similarities | QECC Differences | Advantages of QECC |
|---|---|---|---|---|
| "A Secure Quantum Key Distribution Protocol Based on Elliptic Curve Cryptography" (2023) by J. Lu et al. | Uses a secure key distribution protocol with ECC | Both use QKD and ECC | Uses a novel secure protocol for key distribution | QECC provides stronger security against attacks on key distribution |
| "Quantum Enhanced Digital Signatures: A Review" (2022) by R. Singh et al. | Survey paper of various quantum signature schemes | Both use quantum properties for signature schemes | Uses different quantum properties such as entanglement or superposition | QECC is a promising area of research for signature schemes |
| "Post-Quantum Secure and Efficient Elliptic Curve Cryptography for MANET" (2022) by M. Rasheed et al. | Post-quantum approach for ECC | Both use ECC | Uses a post-quantum approach | QECC is moreefficient than post-quantum ECC |
| "Quantum Elliptic Curve Cryptography for Secure and Efficient Communication in IoT Networks" (2022) by S. Saha et al. | Uses QECC for IoT networks | Both use QKD and ECC | Uses QECC specifically for IoT | QECC is more efficient and secure for IoT networks |
| "Quantum Cryptography Based on Elliptic Curve Cryptography for Secure Data Transmission" (2023) by K. R. Chandra et al. | Uses ECC for quantum cryptography | Both use ECC | Uses ECC for quantum cryptography specifically | QECC is more efficient for key generation and transfer |

**Quantum Key Distribution**

Majid Safari & Murat Uysal (2009) suggested a grounded relay-assisted approach based on the BB84 technique for a free-space QKD system. They examined the function of inactive relays forwarding qubits to another relay unit or the recipient without completing any evaluation or discovery process. They used a near-field assessment to limit the Quantum Bit Error Rate (QBER) of the relay-assisted QKD device. Furthermore, empirical findings confirmed that the relay-assisted approach outperformed point-to-point direct transfer at long connection distances where turbulent impacts are most damaging.

**Construction of QKD by bell levels with non-orthogonal levels**

Fei Gao *et al.* (2010) describe the security study of two to three-party Quantum Key Exchange Techniques (QKDPs). The high-density attack was susceptible to these methods. Eve gained the key pair by delivering entanglement qubits as phony signaling to Alice and conducting coupled observations after Alice's encryption. The attacking procedure was eerily comparable to Eve's with Alice's dense-coding conversation. Furthermore, this assault did not trigger any flaws in the data transmission that Bob and Alice were unaware of. Finally, they highlighted the source of the ambiguity and a viable strategy to improve such procedures in their research.

**Exchange of QKD by an X-type position's entangling**

Gan Gao (2010) demonstrated the cooperative eavesdropper's cryptosystem of a four-party quantum key distribution mechanism. Only one supervisor, Alice, wishes to do Bell state assessment in the four-party QSS method, while the other agents must perform a single qubit operation. The cooperative eavesdroppers for quantum communications have been utilized to prevent eavesdropping. According to the fraudulent actors in the QSS protocol, snooping can be constructed without adding any fault to Alice's secret communications.

**3-party authenticating key distribution methods by using direct and indirect quantum cryptographic Mechanism**

Ananda Rao *et al.* (2011) suggested a solution that incorporates the indirect QKD protocol (3AQKDP) with the direct QKD protocol (3AQKDPMA). Avoids attacks like snooping, man-in-the-middle, and replaying assaults by establishing secure communication. Their technique has decreased the number of communication cycles. In addition, long-term cryptographic keys have been regularly utilized and exchanged between two or more parties. Moreover, a combination of conventional and quantum cryptographic methods can detect the presence of passive attacks like eavesdropping.

**3-party quantum authenticated key exchange technique by employing superposition situation**

Sathi Reddy & Raja Kumar Medapati (2011) proposed a Quantum authentication and key distributing technique to implement key assignment. It also intended to guarantee that the communication's parties were intuitively and formally validated and parties in their approach rely on a 3rd party with only authentication. As a result, the suggested methodology has been used in networking systems that deal with compassionate data, such as those used by the army, healthcare, and research institutions. They used polarised photons in superposition stages for authenticated key dissemination that provides substantial security against various threats.

As observed from the assessment, the initial research efforts have concentrated on quantum mechanics for safe interaction between entities and are particularly practical in everyday situations. It can also be broadly applied to two or more parties, allowing for a wide range of real-world applications in multi-party quantum communication. However, these conventional techniques are vulnerable to cooperative eavesdroppers, resulting in unsafe transmission. Therefore, much effort has gone into analyzing the protocols' reliability. Furthermore, there is no standardization for exploring the QSS system's resilience and overcoming the eavesdropping attack. In this study, the four-state QSS method was examined utilizing heuristic approaches.

### The mechanisms for Quantum Secrets Sharing

Secret share is a method of dividing communication into numerous components so that no one subgroup is required to receive the text, but the complete set is. Greenberger Horne-Zeilinger (GHZ) phases were used by Mark Hillery *et al.* (1999) to demonstrate how they executed such an approach. In the Quantum system, the existence of eavesdropping can quickly identify induced faults. They also showed how to utilize the GHZ modes to partition quantum information into different halves, each required to retrieve the original qubit.

### Effective QSS mechanism using 2-particle entanglement situations

Using four non-orthogonal 2-particle entanglement states, Zhu Zhen-Chao *et al.* (2011) devised a multi-party quantum key exchange technique. The theoretical effectiveness of the new methodology for quantum bits has increased from 50% to close to 100%. Excluding the entanglement stages used to verify the eavesdropping, it can utilize the entanglement stages to generate the secret key. The quantum assault known as the transparent cheating attacker is discussed and contrasted to the quantum key exchange in this type of mechanism.

### Quantum Secret Exchange with Multiple Parties

Using only one non-entanglement qubit, Yun Jin Choi & Young-Jai Park (2011) introduced a novel QSS technique. In this approach, a transmitter can safely convey a hidden message to N recipients by progressively delivering qubits to the following recipient, who can always decipher the information collaboratively after randomly changing the polarisation of the qubit. It also revealed that the QSS system is based on one between a transmitter and two recipients and may be generalized to one between a source and N recipient. Furthermore, the approach is practically possible within present technology because it can use a tiny coherence photon as a qubit.

### Quantum teleportation allows for multi-party interaction

Wang Jian *et al.* (2007) proposed a Greenberger-Horne-Zeilinger phase and teleportation-based (k,n) cutoff point QSS technique for secure direct interaction. The source encodes the secret message explicitly on a succession of particle phases and teleports it to the recipients after guaranteeing the quantum network's security. By integrating their measured values with the sender's, the recipients can obtain the secret messages. The approach is entirely safe if a flawless quantum connection is utilized because the sending photon series doesn't convey the hidden message.

### Mechanisms Inspired by Quantum Physics

Kuk-Hyun Han & Jong-Hwan Kim (2002) introduce the Quantum Inspiration Evolutionary Technique based on quantum physics concepts.

They represent the content in the form of quantum bits in the Quantum Inspired Genetic Algorithm (QIGA). A Q-gate is a variability operation that guides people into better alternatives. The trials were performed on the transportation problem, demonstrating the efficiency and adaptability of the approach. Compared with the traditional genetic algorithm, the findings show that QIGA works well with a low population. The real benefit of an evolutionary algorithm is that it is incredibly reliable worldwide and highly parallel and adaptive. However, the key downside is that verification is computationally costly. The QIGA solved the issue by lowering the population size.

**P System based mechanisms inspired by quantum algorithms**

Zhang *et al.* (2009) introduced the Quantum Inspiration Evolutionary Algorithm based on the P System (QEPS), a new EA that incorporates the concepts and methods of QIEA into a P system structure. A great series of research is conducted to illustrate the efficacy and application breadth for the transportation problem. The findings indicate that QEPS with specific membrane architecture outperforms QIEA.

Real observational QIEA for optimization algorithms and binary observational QIEA for combinatorial optimization are the two types of QIEA. Moreover, $QEPS_m$ outperforms all other algorithms in terms of profit. Also, $QEPS_o$, $QEPS_m$ and $QEPS_n$ outperform better than $bQIEA_o$, $bQIEA_m$ and $bQIEA_n$, correspondingly, with respect to profits. $QEPS_o$ and $QEPS_m$ are superior to $bQIEA_o$ and $bQIEA_m$, correspondingly, in terms of the amount of time that has passed. Out of all varieties of QIEA algorithms, the $bQIEA_m$ method is the most appropriate, and $QEPS_m$ is the greatest of the seven methodologies.

### Genetic and quantum genetic algorithms comparisons

Genetic and Quantum genetic algorithms were compared and contrasted by Zakaria Laboudi & Salim Chikhi (2012). Both strategies were run 25 times and repeated for 500 generations as many times. QGA's global difficulty is on the scale of O (N), where N is the total population. The complexities of a GA will be on the order of O. (N2). As a result, the complication decreases to a linear state.

### Cuckoo search hybridization of quantum-inspired computing for various computations

Abdesslem Layeb (2011) suggested the Quantum Influenced Cuckoo Search Engine as a novel inspiration technique (QICSA). This QICSA is dependent on quantum computing techniques and the Cuckoo Search method. This system successfully resolves combinatorial optimization problems using quantum computational techniques such as qubit notation, observation, superposition of state, and interfering. Combining quantum-driven computation with bio-inspired computation has resulted in an effective hybrid architecture that balances the searching mechanism's exploratory and exploitative capacities. Empirical evidence demonstrates the suggested new framework's usefulness and ability to produce high-quality alternatives to knapsack challenges.

The suggested QICSA effectively minimizes the population quantity and quality of iterations required to arrive at the best result. Moreover, thanks to superposition, interruption, and operations, a more excellent equilibrium among intensity and diversity of the searching are made possible. Nevertheless, some flaws need to be applied to enhance the method.

First, it is preferable to incorporate a local search strategy such as tabu searching into the core of the suggested algorithm to optimize its performance. Second, create excellent use of multiple machines to increase program performance considering quantum-influenced techniques have been proven to operate better on parallel computers.

### Cuckoo search optimization algorithm

Rashad *et al.* (2014) suggested two optimization techniques: a cuckoo optimizer is a heuristic approach, and a Genetic system is a meta-heuristic technique to improve the optimization degree and computation performance as much as feasible. Unfortunately, the suggested model and strategy still need adjustments and upgrades to increase their performance. Nevertheless, the recommended technique is suitable for a wide range of commercial, farming, and many other areas with optimization algorithms; rearrange problem parameters, and you'll have a decent chance of optimizing the issue.

### Tabu search algorithm by quantum inspired computation

Yao-Hsin Chou *et al.* (2011) introduced quantum-inspired tabu searching, a unique quantum-inspired evolution technique (QTS). QTS is known as the traditional Tabu searching and quantum computing features like superposition. The findings of the experiments are contrasted with those of other quantum-inspired evolutionary computation and heuristic searches. The ultimate outcomes show that QTS outperforms the alternative heuristic approach on the 0/1 knapsack transportation problem, with less convergence rate and improved efficiency.

### Quantum tabu and classical search techniques comparisons

Chou *et al.* (2011) proposed a comparison of quantum-inspired tabu search, a unique quantum-inspired evolutionary method (QTS). QTS is based on conventional Tabu searching and quantum computing characteristics such as entanglement. We'll show how we use QTS to tackle the 0/1 computational problems. Moreover, the actual findings are contrasted with those of the initial QEA and other metaheuristics. The final results reveal that QTS outperforms the others on the 0/1 transportation problem, with less computational complexity and higher efficiency.

## ELLIPTIC CURVE CRYPTOGRAPHY (ECC)

In 1985, V Miller (Miller 1986) and (Koblitz 1987) separately proposed the ECC. Using a cryptographic algorithm based on public-key (PKC), the ECC is becoming a more popular approach for safeguarding data from various sources and transmission. The small ECC key makes it more appealing for public-key encryption deployment, especially with low devices like RFID and card readers. In addition, ECC has a benefit over RSA in that the better-remembered technique for solving the Elliptical Curve Discrete Logarithm Problems (ECDLP) operates in complete exponential duration.

### Differential Failure Threats on Cryptographic Protocols Built on Elliptic Curves

Biehl *et al.* (2000) applied the concepts of differential failure threats on RSA cryptographic protocols to elliptical curve techniques. If it can add bit mistakes to the elliptical curve calculations in a tamper-proof gadget, it can utilize three distinct forms of cyberattacks to deduce secret key information. Furthermore, they demonstrate the attack's efficiency in computer modeling with the abovementioned ideas.

### ECC Computation for Error Detection

Richard Stern *et al.* (2007) proposed a Register Transmission Levels (RTL) Concurrent Errors Detector (CED) methodology for Elliptic Curve Cryptographic algorithms embedded applications (ECC). The suggested hybrid hardware and time-redundancy-driven CED algorithms employ the statistical features of the fundamental Galois Field and ECC primitives to identify either soft mistakes or irreversible defects with minimal area overhead. The time yields a traditional approach for adding 2.248 ns, square and lowering 0.0051704 s, multiplying 0.375416 s, inverting 0.98912 s, point additions 1.72711 s, point Tripling 1.75861 s, and Elliptic Scalar Manipulation 424.7907 s.

## HYPER ELLIPTIC CURVE CRYPTOGRAPHIC MECHANISM

Elliptic curves are part of a larger category of curves known as Hyper elliptical curve cryptography, of which cryptosystems are a subset, with genus g=1. Hyper elliptical curves are more trustworthy than ECC since they need even smaller key sizes for the same amount of safety. Hyper ECC of genus g=4 or above lack the same degree of protection as genus 2 or 3 curvatures that have been subjected to sub-exponential time technique threats. As a result, elliptic curves seem to be the most viable option among this group of curvatures.

### Hyper ECC over Prime Field

Avanzi (2004) described the construction of genus 2 and 3 elliptical and hyper-elliptical curves over prime fields. In developing the curve-based cryptographic method over prime fields, building an ad-hoc mathematics package to facilitate meaningful analysis of various groups. Furthermore, use the approach to delay modularity lowering by reducing the total number of modularity decreases in the group operations computations. Consequently, the effectiveness of genus two hyper ECC over prime fields is considerably closer to that of elliptical curves than initially assumed.

### Hyper ECC over Finite Field ($F_P$)

Ganesan & Vivekanadan (2011) looked at the effectiveness of Hyper ECC (HECC) on prime fields of genera 5 and 6. The efficacy of the divisor creation, key generation, encoding, and decoding processes has also been evaluated. Regarding divisor creation, producing a key, encrypting, and decoding processes, the testing results showed that the effectiveness of more critical genus HECC systems degrades. For example, the time required for curvature creation is 10ms, the time needed for divisor creation is 1221ms, the average time for producing key is 8505ms, the encryption process is 8622ms, decrypt time is 10700ms for the HECC for Genus 5 on Finite Field Fp. Similarly, with HECC for Genus 6 on Finite Fp, curve creation takes 11.4 ms, divisor creation takes 1871 ms, produce key takes 9021 ms, encoding and decoding take 9322 ms, and 11595 ms.

## MULTI-LEVEL PATTERN MINING

Extracting the frequency of patterns in streaming data is restricted to the specific occurrence of each item in the set. The usual approach for classifying frequent patterns in large databases is Lossy Counting. However, Zhiguo Qu *et al.* (2016) built a multi-level pattern matching framework to aid the self-directing administration of mobile networks by collecting complex patterns from tele data networking data transfer. Their architecture aids in detecting frequent itemsets across streaming data, the deduction of classification rules, frequent itemset extraction utilizing sequentially and temporal (time) approaches, and the use of dispersed data processing techniques to attain maximum volume effectiveness.

Reza Rawassizadeh *et al.* (2016) proposed various extensible techniques for discovering individual day-to-day behavioral patterns. Multimodal based on the information collected from intelligent gadgets is isolated from these cases. They made most detectors available on smartphones and distinguished regular behavioral norms from temporal refinement, which was significantly affected by the shift of time into happenings. These samples are helpful, including both end-users and third-party providers of data-driven applications. The client obtains control over the information, such as protection, and the quantifiable parameters decrease by dividing the data between devices.

Robert Kessl (2016) deals with frequent sequence mining based on a static method of load-balancing and uses a probabilistic mathematical strategy to calculate processing time. For instance, the methods achieve faster speeds to a reasonable size :: ¾ P, where P is the total number of processing units. Furthermore, the author determines the frequent pattern by using relative supports to calculate the minimum support.

Junqiang Liu *et al.* (2016) analyze and uncover a variety of high-utility scenarios in a novel approach without generating candidates. Their ideas are incredibly beneficial in a challenging and dynamic with a defined strategy and linear information structures. This method aids in the discovery of the reversing enumeration trees and prunes the query region by the utility's outer limit. Furthermore, they anticipated the high utility patterns without enumerating a closure characteristic, also known as a singleton property. Their approach enables us to execute a strict boundary for great pruning and recognize the most significant usefulness instances easily and adaptively, which concentrates on the fundamental driver using previous strategies.

Vincent S Tseng *et al.* (2016) presented a new framework for mining the top-k high utility frequent item sets, where k signifies the amount of required HUIs (High Utility Itemsets). HUIs extraction is a unique data extraction approach that involves scanning all things with a user-defined minimal utility limit, designated as minimum util. TKU and TKO, two powerful techniques for extracting Top-K utility frequent itemset, were recommended for extracting the frequent items without establishing the specified threshold minimum util. In addition, extensive explanations of the merits and limitations of each strategy were presented, allowing for a comparison between the two techniques. Finally, exact tests were performed on actual and simulated datasets to ensure that the suggested techniques worked.

Feng Zhang *et al.* (2015) explored and developed an effective distributed frequent itemset mining algorithm (DFIMA), which uses a matrix-based pruned technique to limit the number of candidate datasets/itemsets. Furthermore, the optimization approaches increase the efficiency of repeated calculatioNumerical analysis, which results in the suggested method being contrasted with the previous system using standard benchmark datasets. It is also proved that the DFIMA is extensible and provides superior performance.

Md. Mamunur Rashid *et al.* (2015) investigated a new type of behavioral pattern known as Share-Frequent sensing Patterns (SFPs) based on the frequency of sensed information for non-binary time frames. SFPs aid in discovering a correlation across a collection of sensing devices, hence improving the overall effectiveness of WSNs in the resource planning process. They looked into a novel mechanism called the share-frequent sensing pattern trees (ShrFSP-tree), which was designed to help an experimental application mining method find SFSPs from WSN data.

Sen Zhang *et al.* (2015) developed a new tree extraction challenge to uncover scarce subtree patterns in a database's labeled trees against a big project and permanent disordered structures. First, they investigated the properties of well-reliable unlabeled data trees and developed novel Apriori-based methods for producing all candidate substrings using two skilled farthest extreme exercises: pairwise combining and leg attaching. They then illustrated identifying sparsely deployed subtrees by measuring the limited distance between a candidate sub-tree and a data tree. These concepts and methods are combined with the frequent originating from a particular embedding sub-trees miner, a powerful technique for handling tree mine challenges (FRESTM).

An effective data structure, Nodes were researched by Zhi-Hong Deng *et al.* (2014) to apply data mining techniques for frequent dataset/itemsets. N-lists and Node-sets require the pre-or post-request coding of any nodes, which saves half the space. They introduced an excellent FIN extraction method, the information for frequent items because of Nodesets. They examined and compared the performance of FIN with the PrePost method and the FP-growth strategy, both of which are the most excellent techniques, on a variety of actual and simulated node-sets/datasets.

Yan Zhang *et al.* (2013) suggested a Frequent Itemset Extraction (FIM) coprocessor infrastructure based on a Field Programmable Gate Array (FPGA). FIM is a common data mining approach that helps locate frequently occurring subgroups from many datasets. Compared to prior initiatives, their technique does not impose size restrictions based on the available components. Furthermore, the architecture scales nicely to many FPGAs and has FPGA rationale resources.

Li *et al.* (2012) looked into the practical challenge of demonstrating the extraction of frequent-itemset in streaming data settings that can suffer from information overload. The most important challenges are frequent-pattern extraction and data-overload management. As a result, a mining approach was presented in conjunction with these two distinct over-load-handling elements. The method distinguishes essential data from flowing data while preserving the data's information model. When the mining operation is described, it is carried out by calculating inexact assessments of frequent itemsets and then recovering continuing ones. When data becomes overloaded, one of the two devices is used to alleviate the problem either through increasing conceptual model performance or reducing data loading.

Tao Feng *et al.* (2011) discuss ideal 2-D (two-dimensional) optically symmetric coding of = 2. Many limitless groupings of deal 2-D (two dimensions) optically symmetric coding of magnitude four and = 2 are interpreted as the result of some combinatorial breakthroughs. Furthermore, the researchers showed combinatorial strategies for extracting the frequent itemsets with varied datasets.

Jea *et al.* (2009) developed a feature extraction method for locating frequent patterns on a value-based bit stream. Unlike the analysis of existing methodologies, their approach focuses on the Approximation Inclusion-Exclusion assumption. As a result, they can estimate item sets inexactly based on data contained in the data streams, and it evaluates the skipping technique. Furthermore, additional subsystems are planned and managed with the procedure for better execution.

Jea *et al.* (2004) investigated the Online Combinatorial Approximate solution employed in digital data mining. Using the exact approach as the Apriori algorithm, OCA scans the dataset twice to find all huge one and 2-itemsets. Consequently, It reduces the OCA computing time, and accuracy remains good. However, the content dissemination of multiple databases may influence the accuracy of OCA's results.

Manku *et al.* (2002) looked at the lossy counting technique, a well-known and widely used technique. It was the first data-stream mining technique that detects common patterns, beginning with frequent items and progressing to node sets. The arriving data stream was split into containers and evaluated for each transaction; the buffer size determined the number of containers. Since the screening of the dataset was conducted batch-wise, the lossy count's technique performed well in terms of processor speed.

Garofalakis *et al.* (2002) addressed data stream extraction in static datasets. Each data element (item) in the bit stream examines thoroughly only once. The multiple data stream results were impossible to handle. Because of the physical memory space constraint, the storage utilization for streaming data processing was explicitly specified and determined. Depending on the user requests, it provides excellent performance for static datasets.

Apriori Algorithm was discussed by Agarwal & Srikant (1994). It was the first simple method for extracting frequent occurring feature subsets. Apriori assisted us in removing all frequently occurring feature subsets from a vast database. However, as the number of data source scans rises, the number of candidate itemsets generated increases computation complexity.

Linial & Nisan (1990) dealt with the approximation inclusion-exclusion approach, which had an inexact unification term value but no readings for specific subparts. It is simple to obtain the actual value of the union keyword if the values of all subsets are known. With the projected value of the union keyword, they generate an approximation count for the common node-set.

According to Shashi Gurung & Siddhartha Chauhan (2018), most conventional systems employ the specified threshold as a constant, which contributes to the problem of false positives in MANETs. They suggested a technique termed Mitigating Flood Assault Method to deal with the problem, which is based on variable edges value and has three phases. First, it uses a few unique nodes called Flooding-Intrusion Detection System (F-IDS) that are installed in MANETs to identify and prevent flooding attacks. The F-IDS movable nodes are deployed randomly to track and analyze network node activities.

## KEY MECHANISM IN MANET

The study (Seo *et al.* 2006) developed a cluster-based approach for securely protecting and creating paired keys for network elements in an authorized manner. Meanwhile, the strategy suggested in this paper has been paired with the Diffe-Hellman technique, which allows the author to construct four kinds of credentials for the network's sensors. However, the network's vulnerability whereby the credentials are exchanged is one of the original study drawbacks.

Another research (Jeong & Lee 2007) was suggested in 2007, in which the researcher designed a hybrid key-creation procedure for MANET while maintaining reliability as a critical element for WSNs in consideration. This study created the security technique in a dispersed nodes matrix environment. Because it uses the Diffe-Hellman method for exchanging keys inside the networking, making the system design based on symmetric-key cryptography via an unsecured connection, on the other hand, the suggested model has split into three stages: key pre-deployment, cluster creation, and key setup among stations in the cluster stage. All three phases have been scrutinized in the level of protection and effectiveness.

According to a practical investigation, the expense of this (Jeong & Lee 2007) recommended technique is 1.3 percent lower than the number of previous approaches hybrid methods for credentials in MANET. The study findings (Lee *et al.* 2008) built a network management system in 2008 to produce a reliable solution for MANET. The suggested approach offers several benefits in MANET protection; one of the essential benefits is providing a secure interpretation and intrusion vulnerability. The author uses different kinds of communication to create a safe architecture: standard and protection messaging. Furthermore, the suggested strategy has proven to be more advantageous for layered sensing devices.

Researchers (Wang *et al.* 2009) developed an ECDSA-based identification authentication mechanism in a study to avoid passive assaults from networking adversaries and authorized nodes using a key allocation center strategy. To secure data development and enhance bandwidth utilization in MANETs, the researchers used the ideas of ECC and ECDSA to build a suggested authentication scheme.

During the investigation (Chang *et al.* 2010) developed a node-based authenticity mechanism using ECC called the XKAS key establishment technique to optimize the effectiveness of sensor network replication. The method utilized hashes with node Identities. The suggested methodology to verify the networking nodes, on the other hand, precluded passively, aggressive, man-in-the-middle, and replaying assaults. Furthermore, this analysis showed that the recommended technique might provide rapid ECC-based computing on a modest implemented MANET for multiplying 160-bit values while consuming lesser energy.

Another research (Yeh *et al.* 2011) developed an ECC-based user verification system for mobile nodes, which assisted in solving many safety problems. Internal threats, forgery vulnerabilities, masquerading threats, replay attacks, and guesses threats are all protected by the suggested method, including a mutual authentication scheme and secure secret key change and updating. The proposed approach enhances authenticating in wireless ad hoc networks while providing robust protection.

Another work (Ju 2012) developed an ECC-based optimization technique on a compact key agreement mechanism. It also incorporates the ECC and DH concepts and a symmetric encryption method. The above technique was created for a single hop networking with symmetrical links between nodes according to the expected and presumed surroundings. The researchers have made a considerable breakthrough in handling the situation hazard associated with corrupted nodes within the network using the system's public key characteristics.

Xue *et al.* (2013) suggest that the protection and verification of the endpoints and gateways must be considered an essential aspect of the infrastructure. This system uses a mutual authentication protocol based on temporal credentials for nodes, with a passcode as a mandatory element for network connection. It can already implement a minimal key agreement to perform computations effectively. The algorithm's three stages made it much more effective and reliable for transmission. On the other hand, the suggested technique is simply for the authorized user to verify themselves to communicate.

The researchers of another investigation (Raj & Renold 2015) did not assert that there is no mutual verification or secure key exchange between the users and the sensors or node in MANET. As a result, the scientists devised ECC-based protection enhanced user authenticating system divided into three phases: user enrollment, verification, and key updating. This technique is compared to two others and aids in protecting the network against various attacks such as hijacked verification assaults, malicious insiders, replay attacks, gateway impersonating threats, and sensors forging threats.

Researchers compared alternative cryptographic signature systems based on memory utilization, memory capacity, and the ability to detect traffic congestion while key creation in another research (Imem 2015). According to the research, RSA and ECDSA are two main approaches to secure a system from numerous security effectively. This research develops the optimum MANET technique for minimizing network overhead and determining the appropriate moment to sign a communication. It's also worth noting that RSA requires a longer key length than ECDSA and speedier computation, and far less storage capacity.

ECDSA has numerous benefits over RSA, according to the researchers, including solid encryption with tiny key lengths, successful implications with compact devices, reduced power computing, low bandwidth utilization, and ease of hardware design. The ECDSA uses fewer periods and executes fewer procedures; however, the suggested approach uses fewer periods and executes more operational processes in optical durations. The recommended technique is a variant of the standard ECDSA that gives excellent protection while requiring minimal hardware. The algorithm's key generation and computation time are speedier than RSA and regular ECDSA, improving the signature and verification process throughout data exchange.

According to Hari & Singh (2016), MANET's protection needs include integrity and confidentiality, data validity, information protection, availability of information, and data quality. These demands demonstrate that there is still a critical have to design sensing devices that can enable autonomous protection.

**SUMMARY**

Quantum computing's key challenge is the reliable transmission. The challenges surrounding quantum cryptographic mechanisms were mentioned in this chapter, along with their benefits and drawbacks. The following chapters use heuristic search techniques to analyze the quantum secret key sharing mechanism and contrast their calculation time and failure rate to current and emerging approaches.

# CHAPTER 4

# SECURITY PROTOCOL FUNCTION USING QUANTUM ELLIPTIC CURVE CRYPTOGRAPHYALGORITHM

## INTRODUCTION

In an ad hoc network, securing data transfer is an essential requirement and an important indicator that works with architecture. The terminals in a MANET are a self-configuring, infrastructure-free architecture used to exchange data over the network. The nodes could be sensing nodes that sense the region's surroundings and physical behavior and have to communicate with other networks regularly (Qureshi *et al.* 2020). Presently, all mobile operators have automatic network provisioning, are simple to set up, and are lesser expensive. The workstation or any centralized unit system is linked to the nodes (Qureshi *et al.* 2018). Throughput, storage capacity, data rate, and battery capacity are all restricted resources for the endpoints. Nevertheless, there are numerous issues resulting from node density, which attracts different types of attacks (Kumar *et al.* 2014). MANET is subject to a variety of security threats due to a number of modifications and constraints. It is necessary to build the best cryptographic protocol and algorithm to protect the MANET connection and solve security concerns (Aliero *et al.* 2020). Because of broadcasting messages to other nodes without trust, energy consumption, and memory management, it is challenging to create or find a better replacement protocol and algorithm in MANET, which leads to high risks such as vulnerable activities, coercions, and various security attacks such as a malicious attack, worm, and black hole attack (Rajput & Ghawte 2017). The major classifications of the security mechanisms are:

- Integrity
- Confidentiality
- Authenticity
- Availability

In MANET, the vital cryptography techniques for encrypting and decrypting the data provide a novel solution. In the encryption mechanism, there are two types;

1. Encryption using symmetric key and
2. Encryption of data uses an asymmetric key.

The key sharing mechanism in cryptography is used to encode and decode the data in the different forms of asymmetric and symmetric key (Wei *et al.* 2019).

## SECURITY DESIGN ISSUES IN MANET

A MANET consists of any amount of nodes scattered in a particular area to monitor the physical phenomenon. The nodes have restricted bandwidth and battery power with a restricted resource that can transmit the sensed or received data. The mobile node operates with a tiny OS used to schedule all the aspects present in the network. MANET has been an emerging trend in the network world in recent years. Most of the research work is carried out to solve the problem that occurs in the network based on node security (Grossglauser & Vetterli 2003). The MANET is very complicated to design the protocol compared to the wireless sensor network.

In this section, the routing protocol is creating a new formation of energy efficiency for mobile security.

The main difficulty in MANET is finding the best route from start to sink node. Many think that MANET is to identify the routing protocol to discover the secure path in the set of connections. However, the nodes are working independently with limited battery power, which operates the key sharing mechanism and finds the malicious attack in the network. The main reason for implementing the routing protocol in MANET is:

- All the nodes are deploying arbitrarily in the set of connections.
- Not fixed location to be assigned for node in geographical area
- Changing of environment is happened automatically due to node movement.
- The node not aware of the location information due to limited power supply.
- The dynamic topology in the sensor network.
- The data-gathering is keep-on changing due to progress of node in the set of connections.

## BENEFITS PRESENT IN THE PROPOSED MECHANISM

Quantum Key Sharing (QKS) is a branch of quantum computation that integrates quantum physics with traditional cryptographic methods. This study uses practical cryptographic algorithms to provide solutions to various assaults, including heuristic assaults and intercepting resend threats.

- Heuristic attack on QSS.
- ECC using QSS based on heuristic attacks.
- Heuristic attack-based QSS with hyper ECC.
- QSS based on hyper ECC with interception & repeat attack.

## ELLIPTIC CURVE CRYPTOGRAPHY

The expression for a cubic or quadratic polynomials f(x) represents an elliptic curve 'E' as follows;

$$E: y^2 = f(x) \tag{4.1}$$

The function f(x) must have no multiple roots for the curves to be non-singular. The formula becomes simpler (cubic) after a modification of parameters:

$$E: y^2 = x^3 + ax + b \tag{4.2}$$

If any elliptic curve has a point $P_1(x_1, y_1)$, they choose to locate $P_2(x_2, y_2)$ so that $P_2 = 2P_1$. This is termed as point doubling, and can be accomplished in the following ways:

Let $\lambda = x1 + \frac{y1}{x1}$, then $x2 = a + \lambda + \lambda^2$ and

$$y2 = (x1 + x2)\lambda + x2 + y1 \tag{4.3}$$

If $P_1(x_1, y_1)$ and $P_2(x_2, y_2)$ are positions on an elliptic curve to identify $P_3(x_3, y_3)$ so that $P_3 = P_1 + P_2$. It is known as point addition, and achieves it in various ways.

Let $\lambda = x1 + \frac{y1+y2}{x1+x2}$, then $x3 = a + \lambda + \lambda^2 + x1 + x2$ and

$$y3 = (x2 + x3)\lambda + x3 + x2 \quad (4.4)$$

Elliptic curves generated over a finite set are used in ECC. Following are the main two different kinds of finite fields.

- Prime finite fields $GF(p)$
- Binary finite fields $GF(2^m)$

$P(x, y)$ denotes positions on an elliptic curve, in which x and y are values of the prime finite field.

The amount of bits in the binary expression of the field order, typically represented as p, refers to the length of a collection of elliptic curve sub-domain variables on a prime curve. The amount of bits in the binary expression of the finite field, often indicated by m, is used to quantify dimensions on characteristic-2 curves. A grouping of degree n can form by a basis point P defined by a collection of elliptic curve sub-domain variables.

**Discrete Logarithmic Elliptic Curve Issue**

The elements of an elliptical discrete logarithm issue are as follows:

- A finite field with a clearly defined boundary, such as $GF(p)$ or $GF(2^m)$. It can use these two distinct finite fields to represent an elliptical curve.
- There is a greater position P on the elliptic curve E.
- A scalar multipliers of P, for example, k, so that $P = P + P + P + \cdots + (ktimes)$ .

As a result, scalar multipliers are required in the Elliptical curve discrete logarithm issue. It's a great way to find given $k.P$ that we have k and P. Since we have to determine k for a certain P and $k.P$, the function becomes a little more complicated.

**More Stronger**

ECC utilizes scalar multiplies rather than multiplying or exponents in a discrete space. As a result, calculating $Q = k.P$ (as operated by ECC) is more complex than factoring (as utilized by RSA) and discrete logarithmic (as employed by ElGamal, Diffie-Hellman, and DSA). As a result, ECC is far more powerful than conventional public-key agreements and signature verification techniques.

**Smaller amount of bits for operation**

Because of ECDLP, ECC needs far fewer bits to operate. For ECC 160-bit, RSA 1024-bit, and DSA (160/1024)-bit all have equal levels of protection.

**Selects Large Number of Curves and Finite Fields**

Depending on the security needs, it can implement various finite areas for ECC. Principles of Effective Cryptographic technique defines finite regions that use ECC. The finite areas utilized in GF (p) can originate from a number list:

$p\varepsilon\{112; 128; 160; 192; 224; 256; 384; 512; 1024\}$

For $GF(2^\wedge m)$ The finite areas employed can come from the list below:

$m\varepsilon\{113; 131; 163; 193; 233; 239; 283; 409; 571\}$

Many different curves can be chosen for the same field by other users. Many such curves and their domain parameters are defined in Standards of efficient cryptography.

### Energy Saving

Because ECC uses less power to operate, it is better suited to low-power systems, including portable devices like smartphones and other movable gadgets.

### Computational Effectiveness

The scalar multiplier is far more viable to execute in hardware and software components than a multiplier or exponents. Furthermore, ECC is substantially more computationally intensive than RSA and Diffie-Hellman (DH) public systems because it uses scalar products. As a result, ECC is the most optimized and effective (efficient) of the current approaches without a debate.

## THE COMPUTATIONAL FOUNDATION OF ELLIPTIC CURVE CRYPTOGRAPHIC ALGORITHMS

The topics explained below provide the mathematical framework for elliptic curve cryptographic schemes.

**Scalar:** A scalar is a component that belongs to one of the finite fields $GF(p)$ or $GF(2^k)$. We use small letters to denote scalars: r, s, t, and so on.

**Scalar addition:** It is the process of combining two or more scalars to create a new scalar. It's just a standard integer additive modulo p in the context of $GF(p)$. When $GF(2^k)$ is employed, we generate the finite field $GF(2^k)$ by polynomial inclusion modulo irreducible polynomials of level k. $e = r + s$ represents the scalar adding of r and s, which yields the outcome e.

**Scalar multiplying:** It is the process of simply multiplying two or more scalars to produce a new scalar. The conventional integer multiplies modulo p in the GF (p) instance. For example, when $GF(2^k)$ is applied, it transforms into a polynomial multiplying modulo indeterminate polynomials of level k, resulting in the field $GF(2^k)$. It produces the conclusion e by $e = r \cdot s$, which denotes the scalar multiplying of r and s.

**Scalar version:** In GF (p) or $GF(2^k)$, the multiplication inversion of a component an is indicated as a(-1), which is the amount with the condition $a. a^{-1} = 1$. Fermat's approach or the expanded Euclid technique is frequently used to calculate it.

**Point:** A point is an ordered set of scalars that fulfill the elliptical curve equations. We represent these components by upper case letters: P, Q, and so on. It will also indicate a point P by its dimensions, P = (x.y), in which x and y are both from the same field. Correspondingly, p's x and y coordinators will be referred to as P.x or P.y.

**Point addition:** Using a set of criteria makes it possible to achieve a third point R upon that curves from two positions, P and Q. An elliptic curve point adding is what this is termed. The symbol ' + ' shall represent the elliptical curve adding R = P + Q, which differs from scalar additions, shall be represented by the character '+.'

**Elliptic curve group:** The collection of alternatives to the elliptical curve formula, including a specific point, is known as the point-at-infinity family, which creates an additional grouping and if the point addition procedure stated previously is used as the collective action.

**Point Multiplying:** $e \times P$ denotes the multiplication of an elliptical curve point P by an integer e. It's the same as multiplying P by e to get another position on the curves.

The suggested ECC-based four-party QSS mechanism will now be described in the chapter below. We can use Quantum-influenced genetics, cuckoo searching, and tabu search techniques to create heuristics and interception & resend attacks. The outcomes are presented as those of other heuristic search techniques.

## PROPOSED ALGORITHM OF QUANTUM ELLIPTIC CURVE CRYPTOGRAPHY (QECC)

The suggested algorithm divides each node into two categories. The powerful nodes in the network are brawny nodes, whereas fool nodes are the weakest. During data transmission, this split of nodes creates a conventional storage mechanism. The next part discusses QECC's incorporation and integration with AWSC.

Quantum elliptic curve cryptography (QECC) is a cryptographic method that uses elliptic curve cryptography (ECC) in a quantum-resistant way. It involves using elliptic curves that are resistant to attacks by quantum computers, as well as mathematical techniques that are designed to be quantum-resistant. QECC is currently an active area of research, as quantum computers have the potential to break many of the existing cryptographic methods.

Quantum elliptic curve cryptography is a form of cryptography that leverages the properties of quantum computing to provide stronger security than classical elliptic curve cryptography. It can be used in Mobile Adhoc Networks (MANETs) to provide secure communication between devices.

However, the implementation of quantum cryptography in MANETs can be challenging due to the limitations of quantum hardware and the dynamic nature of the network. Further research and development is needed to address these challenges and to make quantum cryptography a practical solution for secure communication in MANETs.

Quantum elliptic curve cryptography (QECC) is a type of public-key cryptography based on the mathematical theory of elliptic curves. It involves performing mathematical operations on points defined on an elliptic curve over a finite field.

The basic operations in QECC include point addition, point doubling, scalar multiplication, and point negation. These operations are used to create public and private keys, and to encrypt and decrypt messages.

In QECC, the security of the system is based on the difficulty of solving the elliptic curve discrete logarithm problem (ECDLP), which involves finding the value of a secret scalar that when multiplied by a given point on the elliptic curve results in a known public point.

To perform calculations in QECC, one needs to have a good understanding of number theory, algebra, and geometry, as well as knowledge of the specific algorithms and techniques used in elliptic curve cryptography. Some of the most commonly used algorithms in QECC include the Elliptic Curve Digital Signature Algorithm (ECDSA) and the Elliptic Curve Diffie-Hellman (ECDH) key exchange protocol.

Generating quantum elliptic curve key pairs between nodes in a mobile ad hoc network (MANET) involves several steps. Here is a high-level overview of the process:

- Choose a quantum elliptic curve: There are different types of quantum elliptic curves, each with different parameters. The choice of curve will depend on the specific security requirements of the MANET.

- Generate a private key: Each node in the MANET must generate its own private key. To generate a private key, the node randomly selects a number that is within the range of allowable values for the chosen curve.

- Compute the corresponding public key: Once the private key is generated, the node computes its corresponding public key. This involves performing a scalar multiplication of the chosen curve with the private key. The resulting point on the curve is the public key.

- Share public keys: Each node must share its public key with the other nodes in the MANET. This can be done using a secure communication protocol that ensures the authenticity and confidentiality of the key exchange.

- Verify public keys: Before using a public key to establish a secure communication channel with another node, the key must be verified. This involves checking that the key belongs to the expected node and that it was generated using the chosen curve.

- Establish a shared secret: Once the public keys have been verified, the nodes can use them to establish a shared secret using a key agreement protocol. This shared secret can then be used to encrypt and decrypt messages between the nodes.

It is important to note that quantum elliptic curve cryptography is still a relatively new area of research, and its security guarantees have not been fully analyzed. It is therefore important to carefully evaluate the security of any proposed quantum elliptic curve key exchange protocol before using it in a MANET or any other application.

Algorithm for QECC:

Quantum elliptic curve cryptography (QECC) is a form of public-key cryptography that uses the mathematical structure of elliptic curves over finite fields to provide security. Here is an algorithm for QECC:

**Key generation:**

Choose a prime p and an elliptic curve E over the finite field Fp with a point G of large prime order n.

Choose a random secret key d from {1, 2, ..., n-1}.

Compute the public key Q = d*G.

Output the public key Q and keep the secret key d secret.

**Encryption:**

Choose a random secret key k from {1, 2, ..., n-1}.

Compute the ciphertext (C1, C2) = (kG, M+kQ), where M is the message to be encrypted.

Output the ciphertext (C1, C2).

**Decryption:**

Compute the secret key dC1.

Compute the plaintext M = C2 - d C1.

Output the plaintext M.

## QECC IMPLEMENTATION IN MANET

To make the technique powerful and safe enough to avoid security flaws throughout node-to-node communications, AWSC uses an asymmetrical process for designing keys in the networking. In three distinct circumstances, the network's two categories of nodes interact with one another. Furthermore, the stages of QECC are separated so that paired credentials are produced in the networking for transmission first and then exchanged across nodes over a secure channel. Finally, the metadata on nodes assists nodes in connecting with others; nevertheless, nodes must first handshake before creating a line of communication.

MANET is made up of autonomous devices that are spreading throughout the network. It uses sensor nodes by these networked devices to check different physical and environmental parameters. The gadgets are gateways or end nodes that work along with the entry point to form a conventional MANET. One of the most challenging aspects of deploying an ad hoc network is maintaining topology organization and connection during communication networks. The connectivity of the system in a MANET is impacted by several different elements: topology. One of the most significant and fundamental factors to consider is network topology, as it can affect various metrics in the networking, including data latency, energy consumption, networking time, connectivity scaling, time harmonization, transmission reliability, and so on. The mesh network model was employed for the terminals to disseminate the data with the other's help. Mesh systems generally rely on routing information, which instructs each node on how to interact with the gateway; also, it assists the nodes in directing traffic for them, and that is attempting to go elsewhere. Mesh Configuration has many benefits, including the capacity to travel massive volumes of information around the system, the need for less energy, and the fact that it is regarded as an energy-efficient technique. In QECC, each device in the network is assigned a unique pair key which is generated randomly using a cryptographic hash function. These keys are not identical and can be generated by any node and then exchanged with other nodes. Each node in the network has its unique identifier, secret key, and public key.

To verify the authenticity of nodes in the network, each node maintains an authenticating table that contains a Unique Node ID and a Bit Mask. The Bit Mask is used with a hashing algorithm to verify the public keys of the nodes. A sample of this table is shown in Table 4.1.

**Table 4.1 Sample Node Authentication**

| Node Unique_ID | Bit_Mask |
|---|---|
| Node 1 | 010101 |
| Node 2 | 000111 |
| Node 3 | 110011 |
| Node 4 | 010101 |
| Node 5 | 010101 |

The QECC model uses the Bit Mask and hashing to authenticate node interactions. To validate the information contained in the authenticity table, each pair of keys is saved in an authenticity table on each node with j+m bits on every entry.

In cryptography, a Bit Mask is a sequence of bits used to control which parts of a message are relevant for a specific operation. It is a binary pattern used to select particular bits in a block of data. The Bit Mask is often represented as a string of ones and zeros, where a 1 indicates a relevant bit and a 0 indicates an irrelevant bit.

In QECC, the Bit Mask is used in the verification process to compare the relevant bits of the public key with the expected Bit Mask. If the comparison is successful, the node is verified, and communication can proceed. If the comparison is not successful, the node is considered unverified, and the communication is terminated.

Quantum elliptic curve cryptography (QECC) includes the Elliptic Curve Digital Signature Algorithm (ECDSA) and the Elliptic Curve Diffie-Hellman (ECDH) key exchange protocol because both of these cryptographic protocols are based on the mathematical properties of elliptic curves, which can be used to provide security against classical and quantum computer attacks.

ECDSA is a digital signature algorithm that uses elliptic curve cryptography to sign messages and verify their authenticity. It is widely used in many applications, such as secure communication, electronic transactions, and digital identity. QECC provides an alternative to the current ECDSA standard, which is vulnerable to quantum computer attacks.

ECDH is a key exchange protocol that uses elliptic curve cryptography to establish a shared secret key between two parties. It is used to provide secure communication by ensuring that the shared key is only known by the two parties involved in the communication. QECC provides an alternative to the current ECDH standard, which is also vulnerable to quantum computer attacks.

The QECC model uses a technique called Diffe-Hellman to transfer paired keys between nodes, ensuring safe and verified connectivity. There are more fool nodes (less powerful nodes) than brawny nodes (more powerful nodes) in the network. Each node maintains an authenticating table and stores information.

The fool nodes only record data for the brawny nodes, while the brawny nodes store data for both fool nodes and other brawny nodes in the network. The authenticating table example for fool node 1 shows that it has the Node ID and hash code of brawny node 1 and the Node IDs of all the other brawny nodes in the network. The data includes masked bits and hash code for all nodes in the network.

In the QECC system, there are five nodes, including four fool nodes, two brawny nodes, and one sink or relay node. Each fool node has data for the other nodes, and secure transmission between nodes is established using the details stored in nodes.

The fake nodes (fool nodes) enlist the support of brawny nodes to develop interaction with other fake nodes, and this is done through a handshake procedure.

The sample node authentication table for fool nodes (Table 4.2) shows the Node ID and Bit Mask for brawny node 1 and the fool nodes. The fool nodes have a "-" in the Bit Mask field as they do not have Bit Masks.

**Table 4.2 Sample Node Authentication for Fool Nodes**

| Node ID | Bit_Mask |
|---|---|
| Brawny Node 1 | 0110 |
| Fool Node 1 | - |
| Fool Node 5 | - |
| Fool Node 3 | - |
| Fool Node 4 | - |

In summary, QECC includes ECDSA and ECDH because they are both widely used cryptographic protocols that rely on elliptic curves for security, and QECC provides an alternative to these protocols that is resistant to quantum computer attacks.

**QECC with AWSC**

Ad hoc wireless secure communication (AWSC) refers to the secure exchange of information between devices in an ad hoc wireless network. An ad hoc wireless network is a type of wireless network that is set up spontancously and does not have a centralized network infrastructure. In such networks, devices communicate directly with each other without relying on a central access point.

To secure the communication in an ad hoc wireless network, several methods can be used:

Encryption: The most common method to secure wireless communication is encryption. Data can be encrypted using various encryption algorithms like Advanced Encryption Standard (AES), Blowfish, or Triple DES.

Authentication: Authentication is used to verify the identity of the devices involved in the communication. This can be done using passwords, certificates, or biometrics.

Virtual Private Network (VPN): VPN can be used to secure ad hoc wireless communication by establishing a secure, encrypted tunnel between devices.

Access control: Access control is used to limit the devices that can join the network. This can be done using MAC filtering, which only allows devices with specific MAC addresses to join the network.

Firewalls: Firewalls can be used to protect the devices in an ad hoc wireless network from external threats by controlling incoming and outgoing network traffic.

By using a combination of these methods, ad hoc wireless communication can be made secure and protected from external threats.

Other cryptosystems that do not use ECC have a shorter key size. A significant amount of information/bits are used in a normal symmetric cryptosystem, which is not feasible. Previously, the ECC worked reasonably with a size of 160 bits. Thus according to QECC, there are two stages: it calculates the pair wise keys for the nodes within the sparse network, and it calculates the pair wise keys again for nodes within the network. This pair wise key is exchanged with all the other pair nodes with cryptographic techniques.

QECC employs an asymmetrical key cryptographic technique hence this asymmetrical key is supplied in the following manner:

- Each network node has a public and secret key pair and its Unique ID number.
- Each node has an authenticating table, including the node's Unique ID number, Bit Mask, and previously calculated hashes.

The authenticating table on the endpoints stores calculated elements such as the Node ID, Bit Mask, and hashing code on the network's actual public keys; it keeps those data in the memory region of the fool node and brawny stations. The fool endpoints only store information from brawny nodes, whereas brawny nodes in the networks, as the dominant nodes, store data from both network nodes. This data on nodes aids them in interacting with one another during the handshake that establishes the line of communication. The electronic signature mechanism is based on a secret that is only known by the transmitter. In this connection, the originator is also known as the signatory since it signs the information with the sender's secret or private key. The goal of employing digital certificates in the suggested protocol is to have strong security, i.e., a signing is only legitimate if it can be verified; alternatively, the recipient will be unable to hear the information. The elliptical curve cryptography approach is being used to develop AWSC, one of three kinds of digital signings.

**Proposed Model of QECC**

ECC is the current cryptographic algorithm, and because of its excellent performance, shorter signings, and tiny key sizes, it is a perfect option for network designers. This public-key cryptosystem approach includes relatively small keys where the key is used for data encryption as a public key, and also the key will be used for decoding data as a shared secret key. ECC is based on a solid and structural elliptical curves scheme over the fixed area; this public-key cryptographic method entails relatively small keys at which key is used for encrypting information as a public key, and the key is used for decoding data as a secret key. ECC is a three-step process associated with digital signings that involve key creation, signature technique, and verification framework. The subsequent sections cover these three methods, as well as other QECC-related processes:

- Key Processing
- Key Generation
- Key Sharing Mechanism
- Signing Mechanism
- Verifying Mechanism
- Communication Mechanism

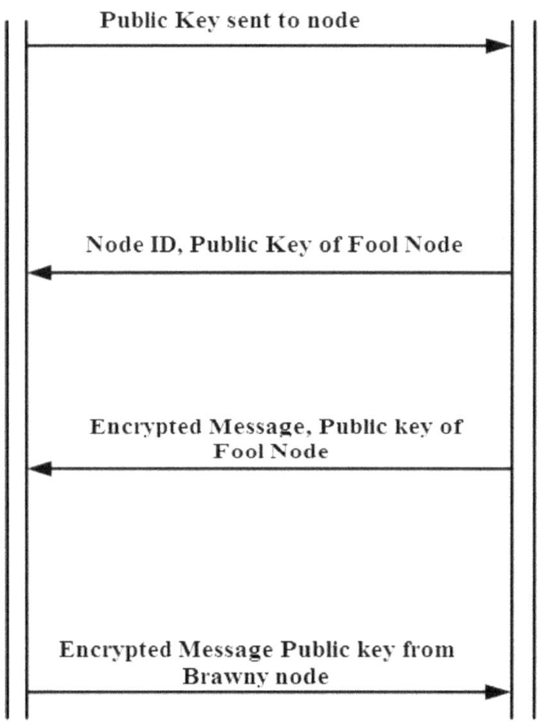


**Figure 4.1 QECC Key sharing Mechanism**

In Figure 4.1, the communication sharing mechanism are categorized into two types of node are there in QECC. The nodes must first validate themselves using stored information as the initial phase. Based on that the communication takes place. Secondly, the QECC technique the node are clustered into two different types fool around node and brawny nodes. In between the nodes the communication mechanism starts to identify the fool node and eliminate from the route.

**NETWORK MODEL**

In MANET, the nodes are deployed randomly the proposed algorithm is designed based on the network topology. In addition to that the nodes are self-configured and it mobility in the network. The projected works of the network modeling are divided into two phase: firstly, generate the pair-wise for node in the network after the key sharing proposes completed and secondly the find the weak node in the network and try to convert the node into strong node otherwise eliminate from the network. These difficulties cause consistent routing to be ambiguous. Therefore, a quantum-based key sharing technique is introduced to discover the solid nodes and fool nodes to find the optimal path to transfer information over the network to reduce the issue created by uncertainty issues.

The node need to communicate with other node first, then it needs to send and broadcast the encrypted key to all the neighbor/forwarders nodes. If a node not even shares the key/message in the network let consider that will be a malicious node. Once the node found has weak node try to change or recover the node too strong to take place in the routing scheme otherwise automatically the node will eliminate from the network as well as from the routing table. In Figure 4.2 shows, the construction of the projected work is follows how the nodes are communicate between them and how they sharing the key information in the networks.

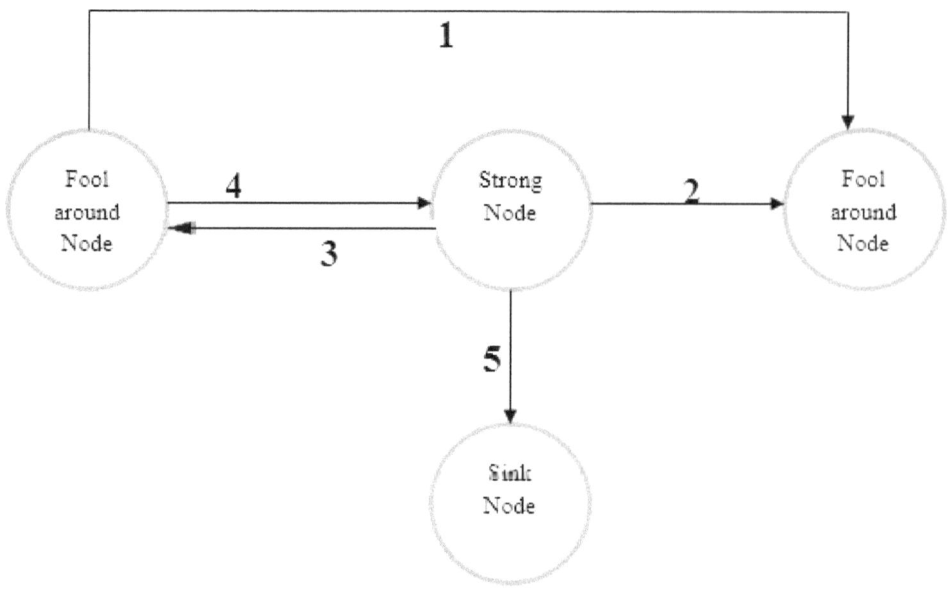


**Figure 4.2 Communication model of Strong node and fool around node**

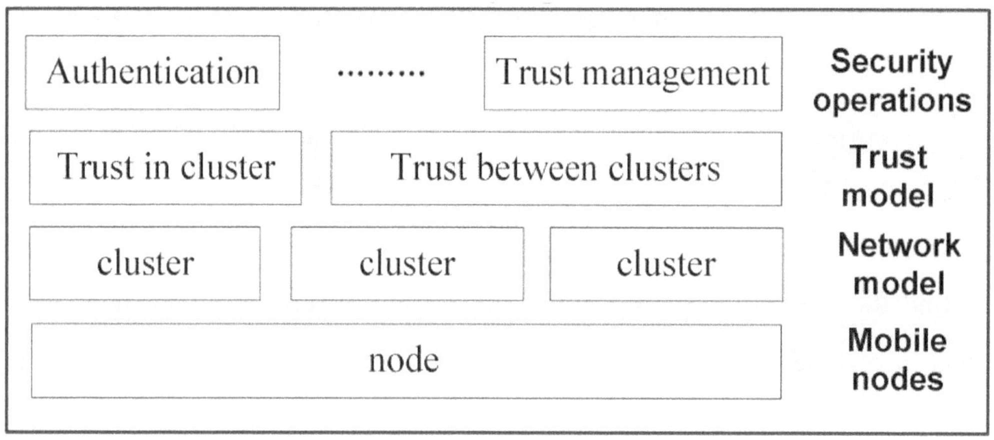


**Figure 4.3 Security Model for MANET**

In Figure 4.3, the security model has proposed algorithm to cluster the node into two set which is already mentioned in the earlier section. The MANET need to create the proposed security algorithm for betterment the routing mechanism and to secure the network from the attackers.

## SECURITY MODEL FOR QECC

The QECC algorithm is proposed to adopt the authentication method and elaborately worked for MANET. The followings statements are implemented to whole mechanism to illustrates the authentication which shown in the Figure 4.4.

- The weaker node suggests that the transmission be adopted in the path by the brawny node.
- The brawny entity requests the fool around node's public key
- The fool around node starts sending its public key to the strong endpoint
- The strong node sends a ciphertext, including the public key, to a weaker fool node
- The weaker fool node sends the strong node's public key, including the ciphertext, to the powerful node
- Verification among nodes is productive

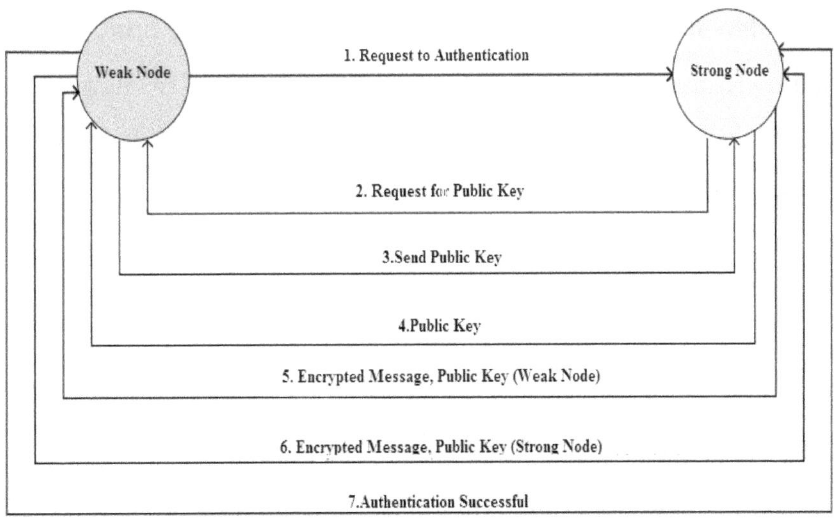


**Figure 4.4 Security Model for Proposed Scheme**

Each sensor node shares its key pair to verify with one another in the QECC. When a node transmits a communication encoded with the secret key to another node, the node requests the shared key. It decodes the information using symmetrical and asymmetrical algorithms, comparing the message digest and declaring the entity verified and legitimate if the digest is exact. The signing is authentic and validated if the comparing digests are identical. It must place pairwise keys on the nodes for identification, and then it can be made write guarded with the use of a function call to prevent access. The algorithm depicts the execution of QECC, with the program beginning by transmitting the public key and Node ID to other nodes within the network and concluding with all nodes being told that communication takes place between nodes and saves time. Figure 4.5 also shows the flow for the authentication scheme of powerful nodes and nodes' authentication process.

The cluster formation function is used split the nodes into two forms to prolong the network security for data packets to form a trusted group in the environment by using QECC protocol. The QECC is dividing the node into weakest node and strongest node, the strongest node only compute the pair-wise key in the network. The key is shared with another node key with cryptography techniques. After sharing of keys the node protocol finds the un-trusted nodes and it eliminate from the path automatically once the trusted path found the data transmission starts in secure manner which lead to solve the problem in the MANET.

QECC work as follows:

- Divided the nodes as weak and strong node to avoid insecure data transmission. Based on the categorization the node automatically eliminated un-trusted nodes from network to solve problem.

- All the nodes have two pair of key public key and shared private key along with their device/Node ID. By using the asymmetric key to distribute the key between nodes to update the routing table. Once table is updated, consider that has to be trusted path for data transmission.

- The QECC function has three fields, key, node ID and bit mask ID is created for the solution.

- Once, cluster formation is completed, the component is evaluates and modifies the path for packet transmission.

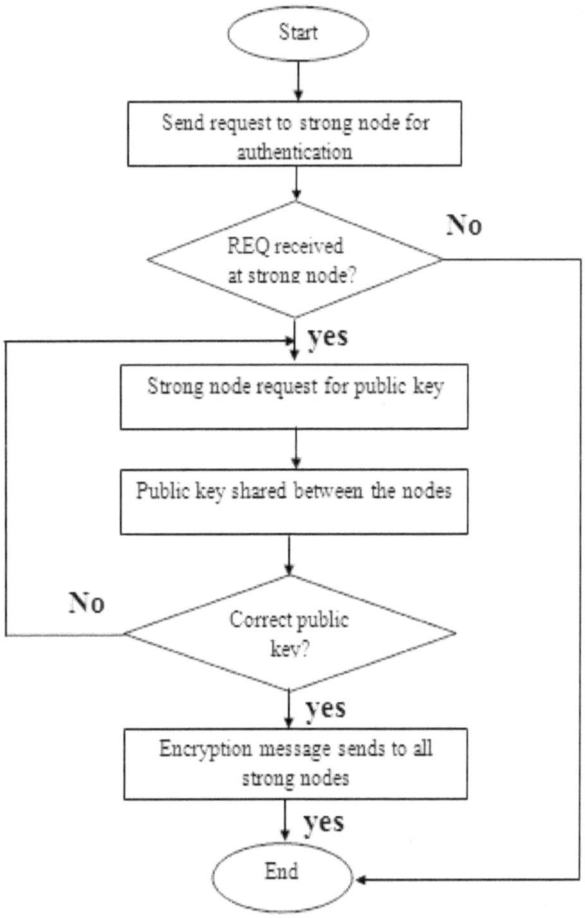


**Figure 4.5 Authentication Mechanism of Strong Node**

## QUANTUM ELLIPTIC CURVE CRYPTOGRAPHY

Quantum Elliptic Curve Cryptography (QECC) is a cryptographic scheme that combines the mathematical concepts of elliptic curves and quantum mechanics to provide secure communication. In this scheme, the keys used for encryption and decryption are generated using elliptic curve cryptography, and then the keys are encoded into quantum states, which are transmitted over a quantum channel.

In a mobile ad hoc network (MANET), where nodes are mobile and communicate with each other without the need for a centralized infrastructure, secure key generation is particularly important. QECC can provide a method for generating secure keys between nodes in a MANET.

Here's a general overview of how key generation using QECC might work in a MANET:

- The two nodes that wish to communicate generate their own elliptic curve key pairs. Each key pair consists of a private key and a corresponding public key.

- The two nodes exchange their public keys over a classical channel.

- Each node then encodes their own private key into a quantum state using a quantum encoder. This quantum state can then be transmitted over a quantum channel to the other node.

- The other node receives the quantum state and decodes it using a quantum decoder, recovering the original private key.

- The two nodes can now use their private keys to generate a shared secret key using a key agreement protocol, such as Diffie-Hellman or ECDH.

- Once the shared secret key has been generated, it can be used to encrypt and decrypt messages sent between the two nodes.

It's worth noting that implementing QECC in a practical setting can be quite challenging, as it requires not only quantum hardware, but also a secure quantum channel for transmitting the quantum states. Nonetheless, QECC holds promise as a potentially more secure way to generate and exchange keys in a MANET.

When network entities of the same type interact using the QECC algorithm, a pairwise key is created for both nodes to create these pairwise keys. Therefore, it is essential to calculate the k-j bit hash algorithm. After producing pairwise keys and hash values for the nodes, they will be checked with the previously stored hashes from the node's authenticating table. A powerful node will play an essential role in creating handshaking among nodes when communicating among pairs of nodes of the same kind. However, this handshake will result in a bit of network overhead caused by extra messages passing during the interaction between two nodes that are the same.

Because of the asymmetric cryptography key creation and cryptographic technique used in QECC, it is secure for MANET transmission. However, if the channel's base station is hacked, the network's security is jeopardized. The previous chapters of this research study have discussed many methods for reducing these kinds of threats simply by implementing an authentication method on MANET nodes. On the grounds of its transmission,

QECC is also evaluated, and As a result, many various criteria have been examined while examining the suggested system based on its transmission of messages, including the following:

- Hops during the communication
- Total number of transmitted messages
- Size of the messages being transmitted

AWSC transmission is separated into communications between nodes of the same type and interaction between nodes of various kinds. Due to the handshake mechanism, contact between different nodes from the same type will produce overhead. Furthermore, because the resilient nodes are accountable for handshakes and initiating network communication in that kind of node communication, it will raise the hop length for the same network by 1.

Contact between different distinct network nodes, on the other side, necessitates direct verification and so needs neither strong node to create a line of communication. As a result, the number of transmitted data is lower during the interaction.

Quantum Elliptical Curve Cryptography (QECC) mechanism over a Mobile Ad hoc Network (MANET) in the NS2 Simulator.

The following are the implementation details:

| **Parameter** | **Value** |
|---|---|
| Channel Used | Wireless Channel |
| Propagation | Two-ray Propagation |
| MAC | MAC |
| Number of Sensor Nodes | 10 to 100 |
| Node Speed | 0.5 m/s |
| Node Type | Mobility Nodes |
| Coverage Area | 1000 m x 1000 m |
| Node Range | 200 to 250 m |
| Data Size | 50 bytes |
| Initial Energy | 5 J |
| Transfer Energy | 2.0 J |
| Receiving Energy | 0.75 J |
| Idle Energy | 0.008 J |
| Filter | Gradient Filter |
| Antenna | Omni Antenna |
| Node Position Update Time | 0.5 ms |
| Queuing Length | 50 |
| Simulation Duration | 600 ms |

Table 4.3 equated the number of nodes and the overall number of keys transferred throughout both modes of communication. As the number of sensor nodes in the MANET grows, the number of communications sent between them will also increase. The table shows the relationship between the

number of nodes, time (in milliseconds), and key establishment. As the number of nodes increases, the time for key establishment also increases. For example, with 10 nodes, the time for key establishment is 1, while with 100 nodes, the time for key establishment is 58.

**Table 4.3 Key creation time for pairwise keys**

| No of Node | Time (ms) | Key Establishment |
|---|---|---|
| 10 | 35 | 1 |
| 20 | 60 | 3 |
| 30 | 115 | 6 |
| 40 | 168 | 10 |
| 50 | 208 | 16 |
| 60 | 245 | 22 |
| 70 | 329 | 29 |
| 80 | 414 | 36 |
| 90 | 518 | 45 |
| 100 | 694 | 58 |

It appears that the time required for key establishment in a MANET using Quantum Elliptical Curve Cryptography (QECC) increases as the number of nodes in the network increases. The increase in time is roughly linear, with a higher slope for larger networks. For example, key establishment takes approximately 1 millisecond for a 10-node network, but takes around 58 milliseconds for a 100-node network. Overall, this data suggests that QECC may be a viable mechanism for securing MANETs, but careful consideration should be given to the size of the network and the time required for key establishment.

**Identifying malicious MANET nodes using QECC**

Mobile Ad hoc Networks (MANETs) are self-configuring networks of mobile nodes, which are connected through wireless links. These nodes can communicate with each other without the need for a fixed infrastructure, making MANETs ideal for use in situations where the traditional network infrastructure is not available, such as disaster recovery or military operations. However, MANETs are vulnerable to security attacks, including attacks by malicious nodes that can disrupt the network's normal operation.

Quantum Cryptography (QC) and Quantum Elliptic Curve Cryptography (QECC) are two cryptographic techniques that can be used to secure communication in a MANET and help in identifying malicious nodes.

Quantum Cryptography:

QC is a technique that uses the principles of quantum mechanics to provide secure communication between two nodes. QC provides a secure method of key exchange between nodes that cannot be intercepted or modified without detection. This makes it possible to establish a secure communication channel between two nodes, which can be used to exchange information without the risk of interception or modification by a third party.

In a MANET, QC can be used to establish a secure communication channel between two nodes and exchange sensitive information, such as digital signatures or cryptographic keys. This information can be used to identify the identity of the nodes and trace back any malicious activity to the source.

Additionally, QC can be used to detect any eavesdropping or interception attempts by a malicious node. If a malicious node attempts to intercept the communication between two nodes, it will disturb the quantum state of the photons being used to transmit the information, alerting the sender and recipient to the presence of the malicious node.

Quantum Elliptical Curve Cryptography:

Quantum elliptic curve cryptography (QECC) is a technique that is used to generate cryptographic keys for secure communication in a mobile ad hoc network (MANET). It provides a method for nodes in the network to authenticate each other and establish secure communication channels, even in the presence of malicious nodes.

In a MANET, malicious nodes can disrupt the network by compromising the security of the communication channels. They can intercept, modify, or delete data packets, and can launch various types of attacks such as denial-of-service (DoS) attacks. Therefore, it is important to identify and isolate these malicious nodes to maintain the security of the network.

One way to identify malicious nodes is to use QECC to authenticate the nodes in the network. Each node in the network has a unique identifier and a pair of public and private keys that are generated using QECC. These keys are used to authenticate the node and to establish secure communication channels with other nodes in the network.

When a node sends a message to another node, it signs the message with its private key and includes its public key in the message. The receiving node can then use the sender's public key to verify the signature and authenticate the message. If the signature does not match, or if the public key does not correspond to the expected sender, then the message is considered to be invalid and is discarded.

It involves combining traditional elliptic curve cryptography (ECC) with quantum key distribution (QKD) to create a new cryptographic mechanism called QECC (Quantum Elliptic Curve Cryptography). The integration of quantum computing in this approach is through the use of QKD, which is a quantum cryptographic technique that allows for the secure distribution of cryptographic keys between two parties by leveraging the principles of quantum mechanics.

In QECC, the key generation process uses ECC to generate a secret key, which is then converted into a sequence of quantum bits (qubits) through QKD. These qubits are then transmitted via a secure channel between the communicating parties. This combination of ECC and QKD provides a more secure way to generate and distribute cryptographic keys as compared to traditional methods.

The use of QECC in identifying malicious nodes in MANET involves the authentication of nodes through the exchange of cryptographic keys. Browny nodes, which are trusted nodes in the network, check the authenticity of other nodes using these cryptographic keys. Any node that fails the authentication process is identified as a malicious node.

Overall, the integration of quantum computing through QKD in QECC improves the security of the cryptographic mechanism by providing a more secure method for generating and distributing cryptographic keys.

In this way, QECC provides a way to authenticate the nodes in the network and to detect malicious nodes that attempt to impersonate other nodes or to inject fake messages into the network. By using QECC to secure the communication channels and authenticate the nodes, the network can maintain the security and integrity of its data, even in the presence of malicious nodes.

### Key Creation Time for Each Pairwise Keys

The first factor on the basis of which the performance of QECC has been analyzed is the key generation time of generating each pairwise keys for The QECC technique is used to communicate in the MANET. The first case is an interaction between two weak nodes attempting to communicate with one other via a strong node's handshake mechanism. Table 4.3 reveal that the key creation time for contact between different nodes of the same kind is longer.

### Count of 'Hello' Messages

The information taken while watching FN1 and FN2 communicate; FN1 is identified as weak node 1, and FN2 is labelled as weak node 2. FN1 transmits a 'hello' signal to FN2, bringing the total number of 'hello' signals shared to one. Similarly, the number of 'hello' signals necessary to communicate among pair of nodes of the same kind via a single robust node will be nine. The frequency for 'hello' signals for various sorts of nodes, as well as the fact that when the number of sensor nodes is even, the frequency is lower, and when the number of sensor nodes is odd, the frequency is higher for a varying amount of nodes, a visual depiction of the frequency for 'hello' signals. The inquiry emerges about why there are fewer 'hello' notifications with even fewer nodes than with an odd number of nodes. The possible explanation for this is that if an even number of sensor nodes interact, there are already several pairs in the system, whereas when an odd number of nodes interact with others, there may be a few unnecessary 'hello' notifications sent during the interaction.

Assume a simple network topology of ten nodes placed randomly in the coverage area of 1000 m x 1000 m. The following diagram shows the nodes and their communication channels:

**Table 4.3 Node and Connections for Hello Signal Transmission**

| Node | Connected to |
|---|---|
| 1 | 2, 10 |
| 2 | 1, 3, 4, 6 |
| 3 | 2, 6, 8 |
| 4 | 2, 5, 6, 8 |
| 5 | 4, 6, 7 |
| 6 | 2, 3, 4, 5, 7, 8 |
| 7 | 5, 6, 9 |
| 8 | 3, 4, 6, 9 |
| 9 | 7, 8, 10 |
| 10 | 1, 9 |

Node 1 is connected to nodes 2 and 10, which can be seen in the diagram as the line from node 1 to node 2 and the line from node 1 to node 10. Node 2 is connected to nodes 1, 3, 4, and 6, which can be seen in the diagram as the lines from node 2 to nodes 1, 3, 4, and 6. Similarly, all other connections can be seen in the diagram by following the lines between the nodes.

In this scenario, FN1 is node 1, and FN2 is node 2. The 'hello' signal is transmitted from node 1 to node 2, as shown below:

1-->'hello'-->2

In the case of an even number of nodes, let's say, for example, eight nodes, then there will be a total of 28 unique pairs of nodes. Thus, the total number of 'hello' signals needed for communication will be 28, and the frequency of 'hello' signals will be lower than the case of an odd number of nodes.

In the case of an odd number of nodes, let's say, for example, nine nodes, there will be a total of 36 unique pairs of nodes. Thus, the total number of 'hello' signals needed for communication will be 36, and the frequency of 'hello' signals will be higher than the case of an even number of nodes.

**Total Frequency of Data Packet Sent through Node**

The overall sum of packets sent within communication between nodes with the same type; when FN1 and FN2 need to interact, they must rely on BN1 for assistance; extra messages can be transmitted while validating the nodes and generating pairwise keys for network communication. During transmission, the total amount of messages sent on nodes.

**SUMMARY**

This chapter proposes a novel cryptographic quantum elliptic curve cryptographic mechanism to overcome the existing restriction in elliptic curve encryption. First, the suggested protocol's security is assessed using the acquire and resend assault. Then, the elliptic technique creates the interception and repeat attack. In summary, QECC helps in identifying malicious MANET nodes by providing a unique digital signature that can be used to authenticate the identity of each node and ensure that only authorized nodes are able to communicate with each other. This can help in detecting and tracing back any malicious activity to the source and taking appropriate action. The experimental results demonstrated that the suggested system outperforms the AWSC in key calculation efficiency and safe sharing of information between parties. - Explain in detail

In mobile ad hoc networks (MANETs), identifying malicious nodes is an important challenge as it can lead to security breaches and loss of sensitive data. Cryptographic mechanisms play a vital role in securing

MANETs against these threats. Quantum Cryptography, specifically quantum elliptic curve cryptography (QECC), is a novel cryptographic mechanism that overcomes the existing restrictions in elliptic curve encryption and helps in identifying malicious MANET nodes.

The QECC protocol provides a unique digital signature that can be used to authenticate the identity of each node in the network. This signature is generated randomly using cryptographic hash functions and is distributed asymmetrically among the nodes. Each node maintains an authenticating table that includes its unique identifier, public key, and secret key, and the calculated hashing algorithm used to verify public keys.

By using QECC, nodes can communicate securely with each other without the risk of interception and repeat attacks. The security of the protocol is assessed against attacks such as the acquire and resend assault and the interception and repeat attack, and it has been found to be more efficient than other cryptographic mechanisms such as AWSC.

In summary, QECC helps in identifying malicious MANET nodes by providing a secure and efficient way to authenticate the identity of each node and ensuring that only authorized nodes are able to communicate with each other. This can help in detecting and tracing back any malicious activity to the source and taking appropriate action. The experimental results demonstrate that QECC is a promising solution for securing MANETs against potential security threats.

# CHAPTER S

# DISCOVER AND ERADICATE FOOL AROUND NODE IN EMERGENCY NETWORK USING COMBINATORIAL TECHNIQUES

## INTRODUCTION

Ad hoc networks are peer-to-peer wireless mobile networks in which datagrams are delivered from an origin to an unrestricted target via intermediary nodes in a "store-and-forward" method (Nivedita *et al.* 2020). There are two methods for securing ad hoc setups. The most common method for protecting an Adhoc connection is a secure routing mechanism, which provides secure data transmission by meeting all security standards. The alternative option is to create and deploy an intrusion prevention device that tracks and avoids nodes that cause malicious behavior in a network. This research focuses on a feasible alternative to the misbehavior of node packet routing. It employs data mining and clustering to safeguard MANETs against message routing misbehavior attacks using non-cryptographic techniques (Deepika Kukreja *et al.* 2018). A node that has been subjected to a cyber attack in a mobile ad-hoc system displays unusual or false behavior.

A mobile network is selected malicious if it exhibits several characteristics: network bandwidth, communication altering, session recordings, battery usage, incorrect forwarding, transmission delay, connection split, packet loss rate, data theft, and stale transmissions. As a result, detecting fake nodes is an important aspect of the system (Aranganathan *et al.* 2018).

Data mining, also known as KDD, is one of the most effective approaches to uncovering underlying patterns in a huge data set (Knowledge discovery from a database). KDD's complete approach aids us in extracting correct data from massive databases. It is a field that involves examining empiric data sets to uncover previously unknown interconnections and produce a new data framework. An essential technique in data analysis is association rule mining. Similarly, association rule mining is used in MANET to uncover frequent node sets, correlations, and connections among groups of routes in routing tables and multiple data repositories, resulting in a massive increase in knowledge due to the data produced from frequent operations.

Frequent node-set extraction identifies frequent node sets that frequently occur in a high-volume data stream. The relevant knowledge is utilized to mine the market database via the association rule, which indicates that if buying some items in deals, buying other items. A data stream is a large and endless sequence of data pieces produced at a high rate. Datastream mining is a process for extracting data/information from many data sets. Frequent dataset/datastream mining may receive incoming information endlessly for the entire transaction, and it can also maintain mining till the whole system transaction of wireless nodes is completed.

Datastream extraction is a fascinating and appealing study subject that has emerged due to its wide range of applications. Data stream research has evolved increasingly important for the information processing, database systems, and computer sectors in recent years. The many tasks in the typical data analysis used in the data stream include pattern matching mining, categorization, and grouping. Information is produced at several terminals (nodes) or remote stations and is continuously sent to a local network. Decision-makers must typically find out what knowledge or information is buried in the data stream.

In a MANET, mobility nodes transmit data from one point to another over the channel, but network nodes cannot know whether the data has reached nearby nodes securely. As a result, the paths through which they deliver data to specific other nodes are monitored, and path histories are extracted from each node's log table to verify each node's routing path. Misbehaving number of nodes are found using route information and the DPCA technique, and the malfunctioning nodes are removed from the cluster by nodes with a decent path history. In this case, mining is critical in determining which nodes are excellent and bad. Before using the DPCA technique, the number of processes and concepts are investigated in the following section.

## PROBLEM STATEMENT

Correlation of MANET and Data Mining: Visions of combination Data mining about exchanges are comparable, to an expansive degree, to mine the data transmission of the node in MANET in the various aspects given below (Jabas *et al.* 2008c).

- For each transaction in MANET, the set of nodes are the attributes and transmission of a packet from one node to another node called one transaction. MANET mining is an appropriate method for a MANET environment with high traffic where many packet transmissions occur.

- Applying the association rule in a database finds all the rules having support and confidence (predictability) greater than or equal to the acceptable minimum support and minimum permissible confidence. If there should be an occurrence of MANET, the standards represent the repeated patterns from all the cooperating nodes or routing nodes.

- In MANET mining, every Frequent Set (FS) relates to one of the paths to effective collaboration in MANETs.

A node-set is an unorganized group of data nodes that participate in transmitting data without repeating paths from one node to the next. Also, data path streaming is a constant flow of datasets in a long series. Scanning the pathways from the data stream produces frequent node sets. The support count value is used to generate the most common node sets. The typical method of frequent node-set mining entails traversing the database, which takes a long time for each transaction. The DPCA algorithm was created with an approximate inclusion-exclusion strategy in mind. There is no need to repeatedly scan the path table because it can quickly find an inexact counting for each common node. Specific additional techniques are used in contrast to the approximation inclusion-exclusion approach to optimize the productivity of frequent node sets.

The experimental results show how attacker nodes influence profile-cast efficiency, which supports our method of dealing with problematic nodes. We require numerous node sets or multiple properties of nodes traversing multiple routes to make better decisions (Jana *et al.* 2018, 2019). First, we consider the mobile nodes' trust as 1 in totally trusted. Further, it checks the node communications, and the node that is sending data in the fraudulent route is called a hostile node, which can be recognized using a true-positive malicious node. Finally, the network is filtered for hostile nodes (Gomathy *et al.* 2019).

These techniques are commonly used in the construction and maintenance of routing tables in mobile ad hoc networks (MANETs).

Frequent n-nodeset creation: involves the creation of a subset of the network nodes that are frequently accessed by a node. This subset is used to reduce the overhead of route discovery and maintenance by limiting the search space for routes.

Skip and complete: refers to the use of both proactive and reactive routing protocols in MANETs. Proactive protocols maintain routing information for all nodes in the network, while reactive protocols only create routes when needed. By using both types of protocols, a node can quickly determine if a route already exists or if a new route needs to be discovered.

Pruning: involves the removal of stale or invalid routes from a node's routing table. This helps to maintain an accurate and up-to-date routing table, which is crucial in MANETs where network topology can change rapidly.

Frequent n-nodeset Creation is a data mining technique used to identify frequently occurring patterns in a dataset. It can be applied in MANETs (Mobile Ad hoc Networks) to detect and segregate malicious nodes based on their behavior patterns.

## DATA PATH COMBINATORIAL APPROXIMATION

The suggested approach, Data Path Combinatorial Approximation (DPCA), extends the OCA method that works at the crucial point. The process relies on the use of the Approximate Inclusion-Exclusion approach and several complementing strategies given by the DPCA method. DPCA aids in the exploration of all possible pathways over a MANET streaming. To estimate the counter of all of the other node-sets, DPCA utilizes all 1-node sets and 2-node sets and the count value. As we perform this with more and more node number levels, the approximations' correctness will improve.

If necessary or if a request is accepted, it uses the registration or recorded data to perform a repeated plan of action to estimate the number of node sets with lengths more than three or four, and so on. It uses the mining algorithm to approximate the counter value of more and more node sets from observed node sets and then provides the resulting count of a frequent node set as the mining impact. By detecting the fool around node (misbehaving) node at different percentile levels prevalent in MANETs, the DPCA technique raises the degree of trust between nodes. To use the DPCA algorithm, you'll need the necessary tables: Path table, frequent nodes table, etc. The entire transaction of nodes is stored in the Pathset table. The regular node-set table comprises node information in which nodes that engage in frequent transactions are discovered and clustered together.

This database contains the minimum support each node provides to its neighbors, depending on each successful process. As more transactions are completed successfully, the node's support count can increase. The node-set is detected and recorded for the forthcoming network operation. The following frequent node sets are constructed based on each operation's clear and distinct perceptions. Based on past transaction records, each node chooses its neighbors. The number of times each node participates in a successful transaction is captured in the transaction database as path sets are used to determine the minimum support. Check out the following transaction table, which comprises 10 MANET node interactions. The following is the formula for calculating the support value of each connection point.

**Transaction Path Set Stream**

The data transfer comprises a series of transmissions with each node in the MANET path table. The sample transmissions on multiple nodes are shown in Table 5.1.

**Table S.1 Sample Transaction pathset**

| TID | NODESET |
|---|---|
| T01 | {Node_1, Node_3, Node_4} |
| T02 | {Node_1, Node_2, Node3, Node_4} |
| T03 | {Node_3, Node_4} |
| T04 | {Node_1, Node_2, Node_4} |
| T05 | {Node_2, Node_4} |
| T06 | {Node_2, Node_3} |
| T07 | {Node_1, Node_4} |
| T08 | {Node_1, Node_2, Node_3} |
| T09 | {Node_1, Node_2, Node_4} |
| T10 | {Node_1, Node_2, Node_3, Node_4} |

**Frequent 2-nodesets Creation**

The initial stage in frequent node-set extraction is to generate a subgroup (Sub-Path). Screening transactions from the path streams produces subsets. Subgroups create when the user does not make a request. Next, we generate the subsets that save in the primary data. DPCA keeps track of all 1-node-sets and 2-node sets in the path streaming. The screening process repeats only twice based on the Association rule method to generate frequent 1-node-set and 2-node sets. First, each transaction in the dataset is scanned to create the 1-node-set. Each unique node is treated as a candidate 1-node-set with the number of occurrences of each node. It is recorded as the minimum support for that node, and we form Frequent 1-node sets from candidate-1 node-set depending on the user-specified minimum support. It retains only frequent nodes in the regular node-set list, then once the uncommon 1-node sets are trimmed using the pruning approach.

**Table S.2 Frequent-1 nodeset creation**

Candidate-1 Nodeset

| NodeSet | Support |
|---|---|
| Node1 | 7 |
| Node2 | 7 |
| Node3 | 6 |
| Node4 | 8 |

Frequent-1 Nodeset

| NodeSet | Support |
|---|---|
| Node1 | 7 |
| Node2 | 7 |
| Node3 | 6 |
| Node4 | 8 |

Support Count = 2

The candidate 2-node-sets are created using a method that joins frequently occurring 1-node-sets. First, we record the supporting value for each of the two node-sets detected from the data path stream. Then, construct the frequent 2-node-sets using the user-specified support value. Finally, only the common node-sets are preserved in the frequent node-set list after the infrequent 2-node-sets are pruned/trimmed using the trimming approach.

**Table S.3 Frequent-2 nodesets creation**

| NodeSet | Support |
|---|---|
| Node1, Node2 | 5 |
| Node1, Node3 | 4 |
| Node1, Node4 | 6 |
| Node2, Node3 | 4 |
| Node2, Node4 | 5 |
| Node3, Node4 | 4 |

| NodeSet | Support |
|---|---|
| Node1, Node2 | 5 |
| Node1, Node3 | 4 |
| Node1, Node4 | 6 |
| Node2, Node3 | 4 |
| Node2, Node4 | 5 |
| Node3, Node4 | 4 |

For support-count = 2

### Frequent n-nodeset Creation

No searching for the transactions from the route stream produces frequent n-node sets. Therefore, some methods are advantageous and are used to improve the mining operation's effectiveness.

### 1) Skip-and-completion method:

This methodology is used to boost the efficiency of the MANET mining algorithm by setting the pace of processing incoming connections. It creates all 1-node-set and 2-node-sets out of each transaction. Then, it stores their count after accepting all inbound transactions from the route stream.

Assume that each transaction is ordered in a pattern-growth sequence by its networks based on that path's historical database. The 3-nodes are created by combining a 2-node-set with a 1-node-set using the skip and completion approach. A 2-node-set is called a prefix node-set, and a 1-node-set is defined as stemming nodes.

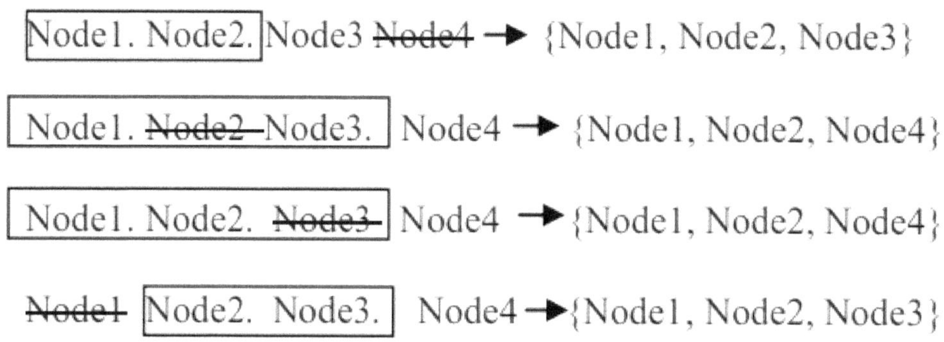


**Figure S.1 Skip and Complete technique**

Figure 5.1 depicts a four-node data transfer. A basic and rapid way to locate all 3-node-set sub-path-sets participating in this communication is to locate a valid prefix node-set, then successively locate all frequent node-set (stemmed nodes) with components of the prefixed node-set. A three-node-set is created by combining all node-sets (stemmed nodes) with the prefixed node-set, and so on. To construct 3-node-sets, the communications in Figure 5.1 begin with the least number prefixed node-set Node_1, Node_2. When Node_1,Node_2 node-set is finished, move on to Node_1,Node_3 node-set, Node_2,Node_3 node-set, and so on.

Even if we do not check every node-set (stems) element of all prefixed node sets in the entire process, we can quickly locate the 3-node-set of subgroups included in the transaction properly and reliably, according to the main notion behind this method. Furthermore, as it does not scan all node-set (stemmed) elements of all prefixed node sets, the scanning time decreases, and the computation time of all entering path set transactions likewise decreases, resulting in improved network speed and performance.

The "skip and complete" technique can also be applied in the context of identifying malicious nodes in Mobile Ad-Hoc Networks (MANETs).

Here's how you can use this technique to detect a malicious node in a MANET:

Understand the basics: Before diving into the details of identifying malicious nodes, it's important to have a basic understanding of how MANETs work and what types of attacks are possible.

Skim the network: Start by observing the network and identifying any nodes that seem to be behaving abnormally. This could include nodes that are transmitting data at a high rate, nodes that are frequently disconnecting and reconnecting to the network, or nodes that are sending data to unknown destinations.

Identify potential malicious nodes: Once you have a sense of what's happening in the network, focus on the nodes that seem to be behaving suspiciously. These could be nodes that are not following the standard protocol or that are exhibiting behavior that is inconsistent with their designated role in the network.

Skip over the technical details: If you encounter technical jargon or details that are unfamiliar, don't get bogged down trying to understand them immediately. Instead, skip over them and focus on the big picture.

Focus on the behavior: Rather than trying to understand the technical details of a node's behavior, focus on the overall behavior pattern. This may include identifying nodes that are not following the expected pattern of activity, or nodes that seem to be engaging in activities that are not necessary or that could be harmful to the network.

Go back and analyze the technical details: Once you have a general understanding of the network behavior, go back and analyze the technical details of the nodes that you suspect are malicious. Look for any patterns or anomalies that could be indicative of malicious activity.

Review and take action: After you've completed your analysis, review what you've learned and take appropriate action to address any malicious nodes that you have identified. This could include blocking the node from the network, isolating it, or implementing additional security measures to prevent similar attacks in the future.

By using the "skip and complete" technique to identify malicious nodes in a MANET, you can improve your ability to detect and respond to security threats in real time.

**2) Node grouping approach:**

It deals with mined numerous paths without requiring a long time to scan each transaction in the route database and control memory requirements at each MANET node. If a node wants to restore route information for the complete path-set of size 3 in lexicographic tree ordering, it must obtain almost 166 million additional nodes. As a result of the large node density participating in the mining operation, the entire memory space consumed by all nodes will be approximately 1GB. It results in MANET memory inefficiency and high storage costs. Therefore, we must construct the system to ensure that the 3-node-sets' are collected to produce the node grouping count values, including memory use and estimate correctness.

After capturing all 3-node-sets:

- Check if the same node-set is represented in the 2-node-set prefixes.
- Cluster by the amount of n.
- Add such node-set count values altogether.

As a result, it combines all three node-sets and raises the count value of the grouping if any member of the union appears in the transaction history. For example, Figure 5.2 creates all four node-sets into a group associated with node1 and node2 and maintains track of entire populations of node1 and node2 in proper order in the transaction (path stream). If any member from {node1, node2, node3}, and {node1, node2, node4} is found in the transaction table, the count value of the group to which the nodes originally belonged is incremented. By managing the information about 3-node-set and so on, we may save storage space and boost memory utilization using the node clustering technique.

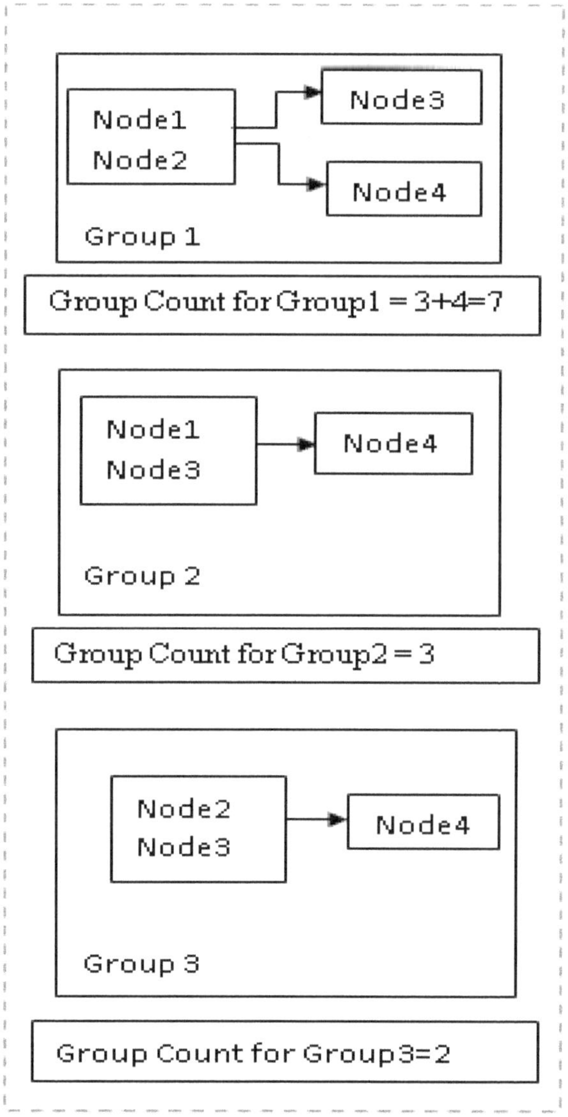


**Figure S.2 Node Grouping Technique**

**3) Approximate inclusion-exclusion approach:**

This method allows us to determine the most frequent pathway from a created node-set of fixed length without repeatedly examining the complete transaction (path history). The idea of approximation is used in this method, and an approximated counting with every frequent node-set is obtained.

The "Approximate Inclusion-Exclusion" (AIE) approach is a mathematical method for solving problems related to the identification of malicious nodes in Mobile Ad-hoc Networks (MANETs). This method combines the concepts of inclusion-exclusion and approximations to provide a robust and efficient way to detect malicious nodes in MANETs.

In the AIE approach, the network is divided into several sub-groups, and the degree of trust of each node is calculated based on its behavior within each sub-group. The approximations are used to estimate the trust values of nodes in each sub-group, while the inclusion-exclusion principle is applied to combine the trust values from different sub-groups to obtain an overall trust value for each node.

The AIE approach has several advantages over other methods for detecting malicious nodes in MANETs, including reduced computation time, improved accuracy, and robustness to changes in network conditions. The main disadvantage of this approach is that it requires a large amount of data to accurately estimate the trust values of nodes, which can be challenging in a highly dynamic network environment.

In conclusion, the AIE approach is a promising method for identifying malicious nodes in MANETs, and it has the potential to significantly improve the security and reliability of these networks. However, further research and development are needed to fully realize the potential of this approach.

The inclusion exclusions procedure is based on combinatorial logic, defined as follows.

$$\begin{aligned} &|A_1 \cup A_2 \dots \cup A_m| \\ &= \sum_{i} |A_i| - \sum_{i<j} |A_i \cap A_j| + \sum_{i<j<k} |A_i \cap A_j \cap A_k| + \cdots \\ &+ (-1)^{m+1} |A_1 \cap A_2 \dots \cap A_m| \end{aligned} \quad (5.1)$$

The Equation (5.1) is used to determine the node-set's minimum confidence count value, where $\sum_{|S| \leq k} | \cap_{i \in S} A_i |$ are distinct node-sets. It only calculates the minimum support for the m-node-set if specified sub-node sets. If any sub-node-sets are missing, the approximation count value, also known as approximation inclusion-exclusion, can be computed.

$$|A_1 \cup A_2 \dots \cup A_m| = \begin{cases} (1 + O(e^{-\frac{2k}{\sqrt{m}}})) \sum_{|S| \leq k} \alpha_{|S|}^{k,m} | \bigcap_{i \in S} A_i | & if\ k \geq \Omega(\sqrt{m}), \\ \left(O\left(\frac{m}{k^2}\right)\right) \sum_{|S| \leq k} \alpha_{|S|}^{k,m} | \bigcap_{i \in S} A_i | & if\ k < O(\sqrt{m}) \end{cases} \quad (5.2)$$

The Equation (5.2) is derived using the approximation inclusion-exclusion idea, and it also aids us in computing the approximation count value. Here, k marks the amount of the information base, m the size of the candidate's node sets, where m=k+1, and S the sub-node-sets. Also, it signifies the linearly converted Chebyshev polynomial coefficient that may be referred to for the various nodes, which contains the first and primarily important node-set, and $\sum_{|S| \leq k} | \cap_{i \in S} A_i |$ shows the summation of count readings of complete m-sub-node-sets with the size of m and $\alpha_{|S|}^{k,m}$.

### Pruning Technique

Pruning is one of the most important approaches used in frequent node-set mining. It is a strategy for estimating count values that do not satisfy the user-specified support count and are therefore considered rare node sets. All uncommon node sets are trimmed using the pruning process, and the node sets that remain are deemed frequent. The minimum confidence count value is a criterion for locating frequent nodes in all transactions' MANET path history table.

As a result, pruning is a potential strategy for mining the common node-set. Trimming is a node mining approach that decreases the size of a path set's tree structure by deleting nodes from the set with minimal power to classify the path set. As a result, pruning minimizes the final classifier's complexity, increasing predicted accuracy by reducing over fitting.

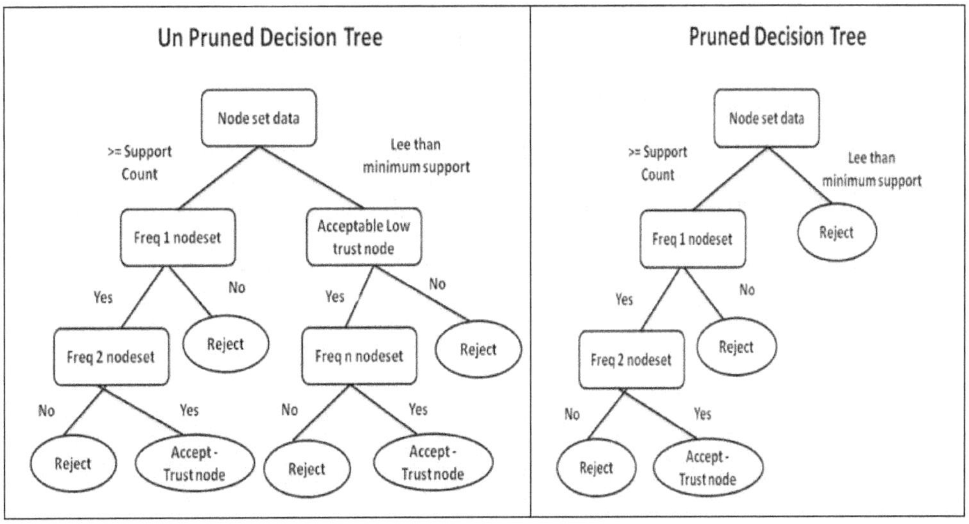


**Figure S.3 Pruning process in node set**

We discussed how the pruning system operates in the diagram above. First, the frequent 1-node sets we form from candidate-1 node-set depend on the user-specified minimum support. The regular node sets are stored in the frequent node-set list only after removing the uncommon 1-node sets using the pruning approach. Next, we create the candidate 2-node sets using a methodology that joins frequently occurring 1-node groups. The supporting value is recorded for each of the two-node sets fetched from the data stream. Next, the frequent 2-node sets are generated using the user-specified supportive count value. Finally, the infrequent 2-node sets are trimmed using the pruning approach, and the frequent node sets are recorded in the frequent node-set list at the end.

## PERFORMANCE METRICS

In the NS-2.34 simulator, the proposed MANET topology leverages the DPCA technique for modeling. In addition, the zone routing algorithm (ZRP) is regarded to add network best aspects of both reactive and proactive route options for MANET modeling and provide expansion support for manet infrastructure. For the complete MANET framework, a modeling area of 1000m x 1000m was selected, with 100 participating devices traveling across the computational model in a random waypoint mobility pattern. On a 100-node network, 10 to 50% of wireless nodes are assumed to be misbehaving. At a rate of 50 to 80 percent, such attacker nodes make losses in dropping packets delivered through the channel. Furthermore, we suppose that such a network contains 30 pairs of source-destination nodes that communicate directly with one another.

Constant Bit Rate (CBR) is a data/bits streaming in which frames are sent at a set number of bits per second. The CBR paradigm is utilized in communication links, which sends messages at a consistent speed of 4 datagrams per second between origins and destination address; we also estimate a one-minute pause time for each operation to the receiver node. The suggested DPCA system simulations took 10.98 minutes to complete. Every network device has a degree of trust of 0.5 and a cutoff limit of 0.4 for freshly entering nodes - the MANET modeling configuration management variables under the suggested DPCA technique.

In the DPCA suggested model, packet drop ratio occurs at various percentages in malfunctioning selfish mobile nodes in MANETs, ranging from 10% to 50%, resulting in packet collision. In the context of black-hole attacks, the recommender system seeks to provide false recommendations for packet losses by wireless nodes in MANETs. This black-hole attack sends fraudulent suggestions to the recommender system, lowering the projected node's trust level (20 percent of the nodes).

**Support**

The part of interactions in a historical path database that include the node-set is described as the node-set's supports. Sup (x), wherein x specifies a node-set, is used to determine the support value.

$$\text{Support} = \frac{\text{Occurence of a Node in an Nodeset}}{\text{Total Number of Nodes}} \tag{5.3}$$

The equation for computing support is presented in Equation (5.3). The efficiency is calculated by varying the support value.

**Base Information**

For instance, we'll consider that the minimal node-set support is 20%. The minimal supporting of an item, which is very well known, implies that its frequency of occurrence must be approximately equivalent to the threshold required to be deemed further in the subsequent mining procedure.

If a node's support is less than or equal to the threshold, it is not considered worthy of consideration. When the minimum confidence value of a node-set is defined as the minor support of the elements, the node-set may be large, but the nodes inside it may be little. It's debatable if this node-set is relevant in this circumstance. In the previous example, the 2-node-set Node1, Node2 must not be considered if Node2 supports 10%, below the minimum support of 20%.

The frequency of occurrence of an essential node-set must consequently be higher than the population of the minimal support of nodes located therein, in any case. The base information includes the common 2-node-set, which is used to calculate an approximation count for standard n node sets. The base data is utilized to make efficient usage storage. The minimal support is calculated using the frequent 2-node-set count of base information. The computation of base information shows that the base information value goes down when the minimum confidence count value rises.

Frequent node sets are formed in the same quantity for the minimum support count of 0 to 0.20, ensuring that the base information value stays unchanged. Few node sets are produced for minimal support of 0.30, resulting in a low base information value. The optimum base information value is found with the minimum support of 0.20, and it is employed as minimum confidence that provides efficient standard node sets for the DPCA technique. Memory improves the DPCA algorithm's performance significantly. The memory of the DPCA algorithm is increased by leveraging the base information, which eliminates the need for continuous node-set scanning. The reaction time is also enhanced because the DPCA algorithm builds the common node-set from the information base.

By clustering the fool around network nodes, we may exclude them from contributing to the routing mechanism using the DPCA approach.

The frequent operations are extracted by the DPCA technique based on transaction records at each node faster by the Node aggregation method without screening all the transactions continually. The DPCA approach also identifies the proactive nodes in the network that regularly complete transactions, allowing only the active nodes to participate in interaction and defend the MANET.

## SUMMARY

Using the Data Path Combinatorial Approximations (DPCA) methodology, the entire section works with a frequent node collection from a MANET dataset. Nodes that do not frequently set delivery are prohibited and inspected more closely. To determine the approximate counting of standard node sets, the approximation inclusion-exclusion method, skip and complete methodology, and group count methodology was used - the DPCA, which was used to examine the Paths indefinitely. The skip and completion strategy helped to shorten responsiveness. The lexicographic ordering prefix tree was employed in the group count approach to express frequent node sets. In the next section, 6, the findings are explained in-depth, and the method's previous experience is addressed using Ns-2 simulator. Finally, the DPCA finds and maintains a solution to a problem. The DPCA may generate energy consumption given a node's lower power, failure rate, and trustworthy route.

# CHAPTER 6

# RESULT AND DISCUSSIONS

## INTRODUCTION

This chapter explains how to interpret the modeling results obtained using quantum elliptic curve cryptography to design a routing scheme with excellent connectivity. The nodes are placed throughout the surface area to ensure that the collected data is transferred quickly - the data transmission securely from the source to the sink. The QECC's performance has been evaluated using the primary key method. First, the QECC generates the pair-wise key for MANET. Then, the network first classifies the node into two types: weak and robust nodes. The vulnerable nodes attempt to connect, but the network identifies the untrustworthy node and removes it from the table. The result reveals that it takes longer to generate a key for communication between two nodes of the same kind.

## SOFTWARE SPECIFICATION

In the networking area there are many simulators are available such as NS-2, OMNET, GLOMOSIM, Qual-Net, OPNet, etc. The researchers need to simulate and evaluate the protocol, algorithms, data packet size, node utilization.

**Network Simulator-2 Software**

The Network Simulator version 2(NS-2) is discrete event-driven simulation software specially made for wireless sensor network. It is UNIX based package that shows the performance and behaviour of network communication of both wired and wireless network. The NS-2 is language which differs from high level language called as Tool Command Language (TCL) script. The network simulator implements in various protocol such as TCP, UDP, CBR, SINK, VBF, DBR, ect., to manage the route in the simulator. In general, NS2 provides user to specify the protocol specification and behaviours of the node in the network. The simulator basic architecture show in the Figure 6.1.

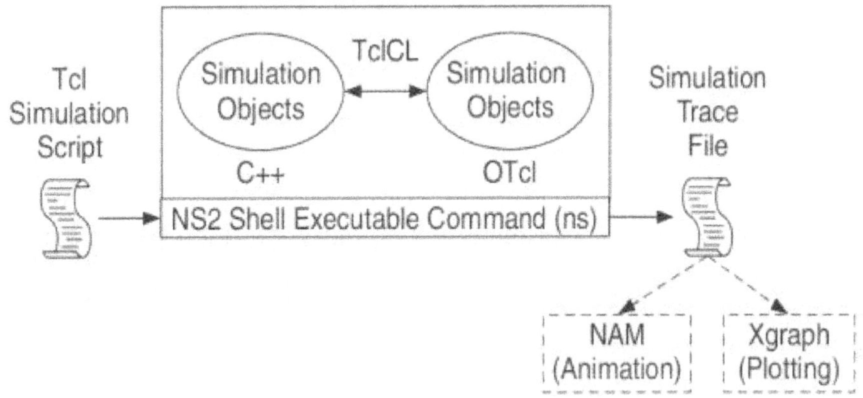


**Figure 6.1 Basic Architecture of NS2**

The NS2 is other word is Object Oriented Tcl (OTcl). The NS2 work with two major languages: C++ and OTcl. The C++ language used to maintain the header file and class file of simulator to perform well in the output. The NS2 creates the file in OTcl script format example filename.tcl which used to run simulator, the C++ code is used to compile the tcl script to execute the configuration, setup, and time management of the simulation which shows in the Figure 6.2.

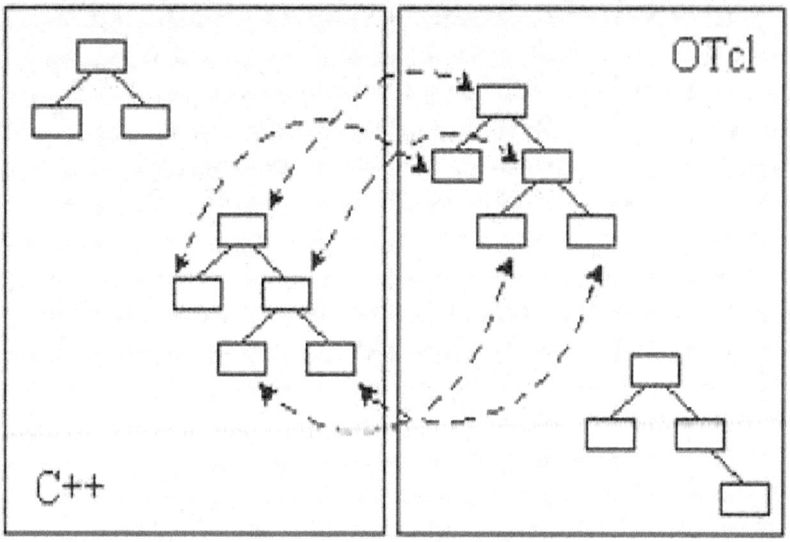


**Figure 6.2 C++ and OTCL duality**

The main component of the NS2 is Network Animator file (NAM), Xgraph file, Trace file (.tr), to analysis the network performance by these components. The NAM file is a graphical user interface which used to visualize the network performance is similarly as video player (Play, pause, fast forward, rewind, zoom in zoom out etc.). The Xgraph is used to plot the graph to analysis the packet delivery, delay time taken to complete the transmission with help of trace file. In trace file it trace all event schedule in the network and performance of the routing function, data drop, size of packet send and throughput etc.

**Features of NS2**

The NS2 is difficult to implement the network scenario to test. The results can obtain quickly in minimum time duration which helps to configure are modified the protocol as won creation. The NS2 is the best of the researchers community that performance well to simulate and analysis the script.

**Advantages:**

- Free of Cost it doesn't required any Hardware
- Execution obtain quickly
- Testing compactable
- User friendly
- Add own protocol
- More popular and modularity

**Disadvantages:**

- Real system too complex to model. i.e. complicated structure.
- Bugs are unreliable

## PERFORMANCE ANALYSIS OF QECC FUNCTION

The Quantum Elliptic Curve Cryptography (QECC) is simulated in the NS2 is used to perform in the routing protocol. There are 100 nodes were deployed in the various depth and the transmission range is 1000mx1000m with random point. The performances of the various data packets are analyzed and calculated throughput and error rate were examined to attain the result such as energy consumption, packet delivery ratio and trust level

Based on the table the number of nodes, routing protocol, data transmission and simulation are used to test the network performance with help QECC algorithm. In, all the aspects the simulation testing result is taken. The results is analyzed with the existing protocol are explained in the upcoming topic.

**Table 6.1 Parameters and Simulation Setup for QECC**

| Channel Used | Wireless Channel |
|---|---|
| Propagation | Two ray Propagation |
| MAC | MAC |
| No. of Sensor Node deployed | 100 to 1000 |
| Speed of the node in water | 0.5 |
| Nodes | Mobility nodes |
| Coverage | 1000 X 1000 $m^2$ |
| Node Range | 200 to 250 m |
| Data Size | 50 bytes |
| Initial Energy | 5 J |
| Transfer energy | 2.0 |
| Receiving energy | 0.75 |
| Idle energy | 0.008 |
| Filter | Gradient Filter |
| Antenna | Omni Antenna |
| Node Position updates (interval time) | 0.5ms |
| Queuing Length | 50 |
| Simulation Duration | 600ms |

**Variation of Average Key Generation for QECC Vs AWSC**

The number or node used in different area the data transmission from source to destination. By using elliptical curve structure for key sharing in the networks.

In Figure 6.3 examined the performance of both QECC and AWSC. The key creation time of producing each paired key for transmission in an ad hoc network of the QECC system was examined as the basic efficiency of the

QECC. The first situation of the scheme is to set the communication between the fool around node and strong node.

**Table 6.2 Average Key Generation for GDPT Vs GFGD**

| Nodes | Average Key Generation | |
|---|---|---|
| | AWSC | QECC |
| 10 | 60 | 45 |
| 20 | 158 | 126 |
| 30 | 310 | 289 |
| 40 | 468 | 398 |
| 50 | 580 | 545 |
| 60 | 631 | 622 |
| 70 | 765 | 740 |
| 80 | 777 | 756 |
| 90 | 823 | 798 |
| 100 | 876 | 836 |

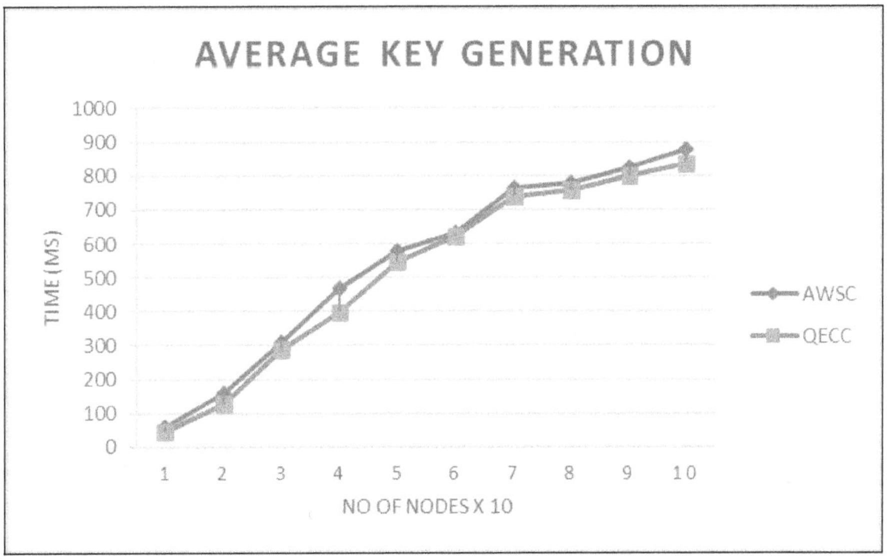


**Figure 6.3 Average Key Generation**

The fool node not able to get the route information because it considered as malicious node in the networks. The fool node are trying to communicate with each other which helps of handshaking process to brawny node. The outcomes revealed the time it takes to generate a key for network communication. Using the asymmetric algorithm, the QECC has the best chance of discovering a route and determining the next hop. Changes in node and path will be considered while generating pair-wise keys.

### Variations of Average Count of "Hello Message for QECC Vs AWSC

The result shows the number of hello message is sent to the sink node in secured communication between the forwarded nodes. The result is plotted based on simulation test. The Table 6.3 represents the number of node used and count of the hello message sent.

**Table 6.3 Average Count of "Hello" Message for QECC Vs AWSC**

| Nodes | Hello Message | |
|---|---|---|
| | QECC | AWSC |
| 10 | 1 | 1 |
| 20 | 3 | 3 |
| 30 | 6 | 5 |
| 40 | 10 | 8 |
| 50 | 16 | 12 |
| 60 | 22 | 18 |
| 70 | 29 | 23 |
| 80 | 36 | 28 |
| 90 | 45 | 37 |
| 100 | 58 | 44 |

In Table 6.2 shows that the Average count of the hello message exchanged between the selected nodes. This is because of virtual location of nodes in the network are selected for packet transmission between source and destination. In this, the malicious nodes selects the fool node to retrieve the data in this simulation the node are secure and transmitted the data via trusted path to reach the sink node safely and based on this the error rate also calculated and packet are directly sent to particular node which is called brawny node to sink node. So, the packet delivery ratio remains same between source and destination and security of the data also improved by using QECC when compare to AWSC.

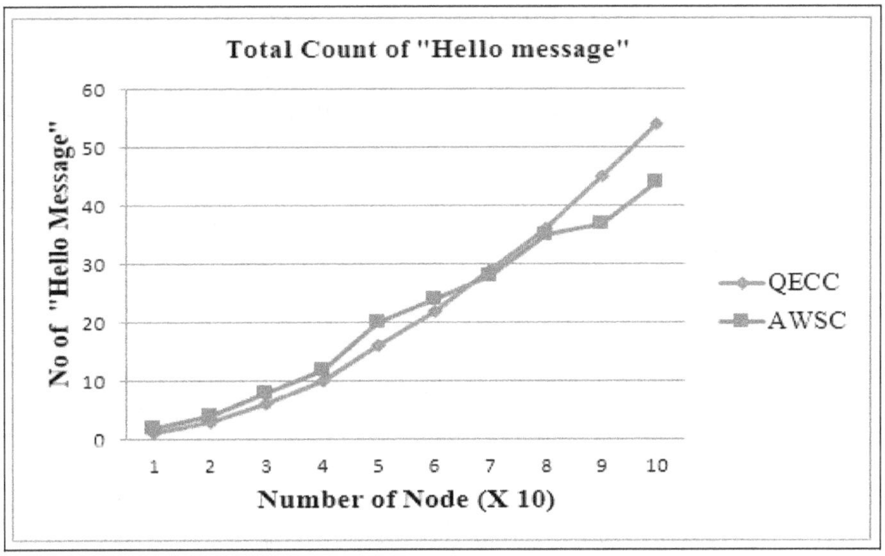


**Figure 6.4 Average Count of "Hello Message"**

The data acquired between the source and destination and the sinking node is represented in Figure 6.4, where the sender delivers the data to the base station via intermediates. The sender forwards a 'hello' signal to the sink, transferring the total number of 'hello' signals to one. Similarly, the number of 'hello' signals necessary to communicate among pair of nodes of the same kind via a brawny node will be 6. Table 6.3 indicates the frequency for 'hello' signals for various network nodes, as well as the fact that when the number of sensor nodes is even, the count is lower, and when the number of sensor nodes is odd, the count is higher. Figure 10 provides a schematic representation of the amount of 'hello' communications sent for various numbers of nodes.

### Variations of Average Error Rate for QECC Vs AWSC

We calculate the failure rate by altering the node mobility between static to dynamical topological changes and network movement. The Table 6.4 shows the average error rate.

**Table 6.4 Average Error Rate for QECC Vs AWSC**

| Nodes | Error Rate | |
|---|---|---|
| | QECC | AWSC |
| 10 | 5.00 | 8.00 |
| 20 | 6.20 | 9.12 |
| 30 | 8.04 | 10.71 |
| 40 | 8.31 | 12.71 |
| 50 | 9.85 | 13.01 |
| 60 | 10.19 | 14.06 |
| 70 | 11.21 | 13.11 |
| 80 | 10.92 | 12.90 |
| 90 | 9.65 | 12.33 |
| 100 | 9.32 | 12.34 |

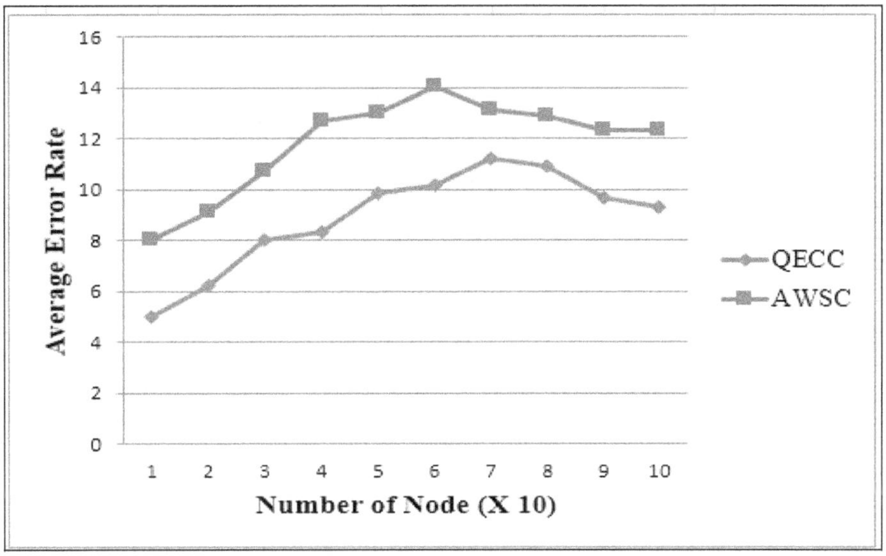


**Figure 6.5 Average Error Rate**

The symmetrical and asymmetrical algorithms improve the node density to locate more trusted paths, as seen in Figure 4.5. The brawny and source nodes are more likely to discover the next node in the network for the location using the Distance measure. By shifting the node migration from static to highly dynamic topologies and node mobility, we simulated packet quality, which reveals that ad hoc networks have a higher success rate than QECC. Furthermore, the symmetrical and asymmetrical functions rely on the fool node to turn into a powerful node and transmit messages to the sinks.

**Variations of Average Trust Path for QECC Vs AWSC**

By altering the node motion from stationary to the rapid evolution of architecture and locating the brawny node in the networks, the simulation is carried out for the edge node. The average percentage of routing nodes within the network is shown in Table 6.4, and the computation for determining the trust path is dependent on that.

**Table 6.5 Average Trust Path for QECC Vs AWSC**

| Nodes | Trust Path | |
|---|---|---|
| | QECC | AWSC |
| 10 | 0 | 1 |
| 20 | 1.2 | 1 |
| 30 | 1.5 | 1 |
| 40 | 3 | 1.1 |
| 50 | 4.2 | 1 |
| 60 | 4.7 | 1 |
| 70 | 6.2 | 1.1 |
| 80 | 7.5 | 1.2 |
| 90 | 7.9 | 2 |
| 100 | 10 | 2 |

The table shows the trust path of each node in the network using both QECC and AWSC, where a lower trust path value indicates a higher level of trust. Based on this information, we can see that in the QECC column, the trust path values are generally lower than those in the AWSC column. This means that the nodes in the network have a higher level of trust in each other when using QECC as compared to AWSC.

The use of QECC helps in identifying malicious nodes in the network by providing a unique digital signature that can be used to authenticate the identity of each node and ensure that only authorized nodes are able to communicate with each other. In the case of the above table, we can see that the trust path values for nodes 40 and 70 are higher when using AWSC as compared to QECC. This indicates that these nodes may not be as trustworthy in the network when using AWSC.

With the help of QECC, any malicious activity can be detected and traced back to the source node based on the unique digital signature. This is because QECC provides a more secure and efficient way of sharing keys and authenticating the identity of each node. Therefore, the use of QECC can help to improve the security of the MANET and reduce the risk of malicious attacks.

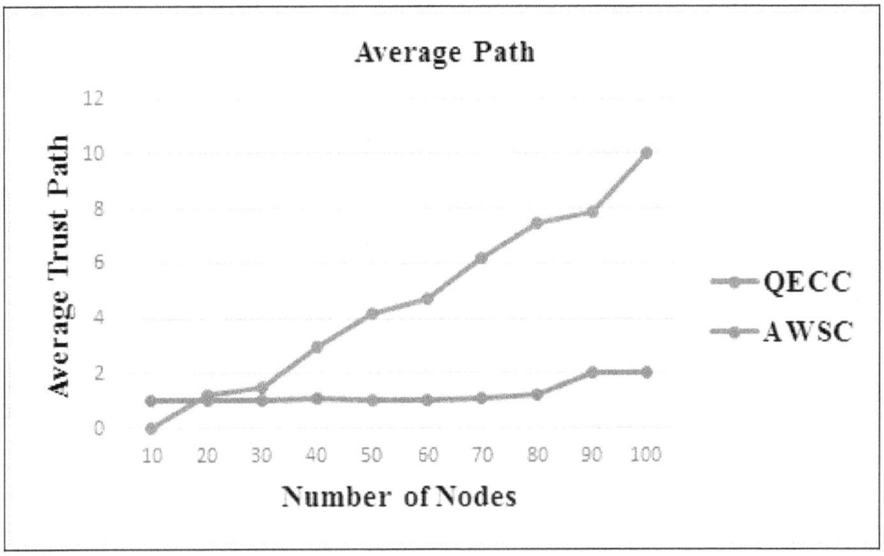


**Figure 6.6 Average Trusted Path**

In each node in the network has a trust path value assigned for both QECC and AWSC. This value represents the level of trust assigned to the node based on its previous interactions and communications within the network.

When a new node attempts to join the network, it must first be authenticated and authorized by the existing nodes. In the case of QECC, this authentication is done using the unique digital signature provided by the QECC protocol, which helps to ensure that only authorized nodes are able to join the network.

Once a new node has been authorized and added to the network, the brawny and source nodes can use the distance measure and key authentication generated by QECC to discover the next node in the network and communicate with it securely. Any node that fails to provide the appropriate authentication and encryption key generated by QECC will not be able to communicate with the rest of the network.

In contrast, AWSC uses ECC for key generation and authentication, which may not provide the same level of security as QECC. Additionally, the trust path values assigned to nodes in the AWSC network may not be as accurate or reliable as those assigned in the QECC network, which could result in a higher risk of malicious nodes being able to join and operate undetected.

Overall, the use of QECC in MANETs can provide a more secure and reliable means of identifying and authenticating nodes, which can help to prevent malicious nodes from entering the network and carrying out attacks.

**Overall Percentage Comparison of proposed QECC and AWSC with all Results**

**Table 6.6 Overall Percentage Comparison with all Parameter Results**

| Quality Parameter | QECC | AWSC |
|---|---|---|
| Key Generation | 58 | 54.5 |
| Packet Sent | 57.14 | 42.86 |
| Error rate | 9.85 | 13.01 |
| Trusted Path | 4.2 | 1 |

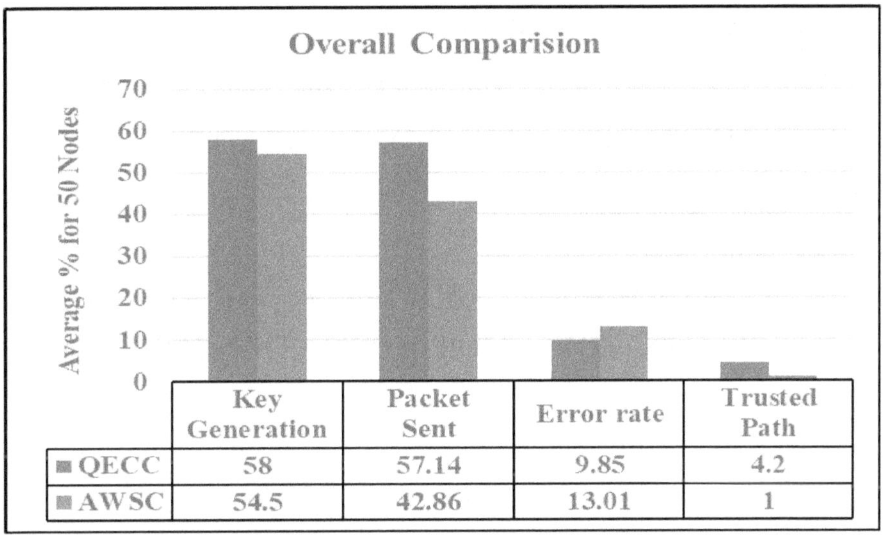


**Figure 6.7 Overall Percentage Comparison with all Parameter results**

**Key Generation:** The average key generated in QECC nearly 46% more than AWSC value only 32%. When the node increased pairwise key also increased, in QECC the source node decision made based on the brawny node which is need to convert the fool node to strong node for data transmission.

**Packet Sent:** The packet sent ratio is increased based on the message count between the nodes. The simulation result shows that QECC increase the value by 68% approximately when compared to AWSC in that only 58% of packet sent to sink node. The secured packet successfully sent high in the QECC. Hence the mobility of nodes also calculated. The High Packet delivery ratio is increased in the given result

**Error Rate:** The simulation result shows the approximate value 48% in QECC it compared with AWSC the result shows the value is 69% error in delivered packet. The error is occurs due to fool node and the conversion of fool node to strong node it increased the energy of a node by reducing the fool node in communication. The result shows the success of the error rate is decreased in QECC.

**Trusted Path:** The average of trust path value in QECC nearly 46% more than AWSC value only 32%. When the brawny node increased, the path also increased, in QECC the route decision made based on the source node which is near to sink node.

## PERFORMANCE ANALYSIS OF DATA PATH COMBINATORIAL APPROXIMATION PROTOCOL

The performance analysis of Data Path Combinatorial Approximation protocol results were discussed detailed in this section. The deployment of the nodes in different area it used to transmit the data from source to sink node. The area of the network coverage is 1000 x 1000 $m^2$. The measurements details described in the below Table 6.7.

**Table 6.7 Parameters and Simulation Setup for DPCA**

| Simulation Parameters | Value |
|---|---|
| No of wireless nodes | 100 |
| Modeling area | 1000m x 1000m |
| Node movement | 10 m/s |
| Transmission coverage | 250 m |
| Model of movement | Random Waypoint Model |
| Routing scheme | ZRP |
| Pair nodes - sender to receiver | 30 |
| Channel capacity | 2 Kbps |
| Model of Traffic | CBR model |
| Payload size | 512 Bytes |
| Computational time | 500s |
| Maximum threshold | 0.5 |
| Trust node threshold | 0.4 |
| Pause interval | 1min |

**Performance of DPCA**

Three Quality criteria, including performance, energy usage, and packet drop, evaluate the DPCA suggested approach. In the existence of malicious nodes, the recommended DPCA method is modeled between MANET nodes. The proposed DPCA paradigm in MANET network infrastructure that assesses a node's trustworthiness is tested in three situations, which are listed below:

**Situation 1:** Packets are transmitted using the ZRP routing scheme, and participating nodes have no trust relationships (or) fail to send packets frequently.

**Situation 2:** Packets are transmitted using the ZRP routing mechanism and the DPCA technique by nodes in the network, with frequent successful transactions to other nodes.

**Situation 3:** Packets are transmitted using the ZRP routing algorithm, and network nodes have suggested a DPCA trustworthy relationship based on repeated successful transactions to other nodes.

The actual effect of compromised nodes on performance measures is depicted in the figures below. The experimental outcome of the compromised nodes was presented in this section, which impacted several performance measures like performance, packet drop, and energy usage. The performance measures are studied at different proportions of fool-around (malicious/selfish) nodes, ranging between 10% to 40%.

Figure 6.8 shows the overall throughput result in MANETs in the existence of black-hole compromised nodes. In the presence of different nodes, the graph presents the performance results in a continuous declining fashion. According to the graph plot, situation 3 has a greater throughput level, situation 2 has a moderate throughput level, and situation 1 has the lowest throughput. In the existence of a fool-around node/mischievous nodes and the Zone routing algorithm, the DPCA technique achieves better throughput than the other approaches. Figure 6.8 shows the results of packet drop experiments in the presence of a fool around node (mischievous) node at different percentile levels in MANETs.

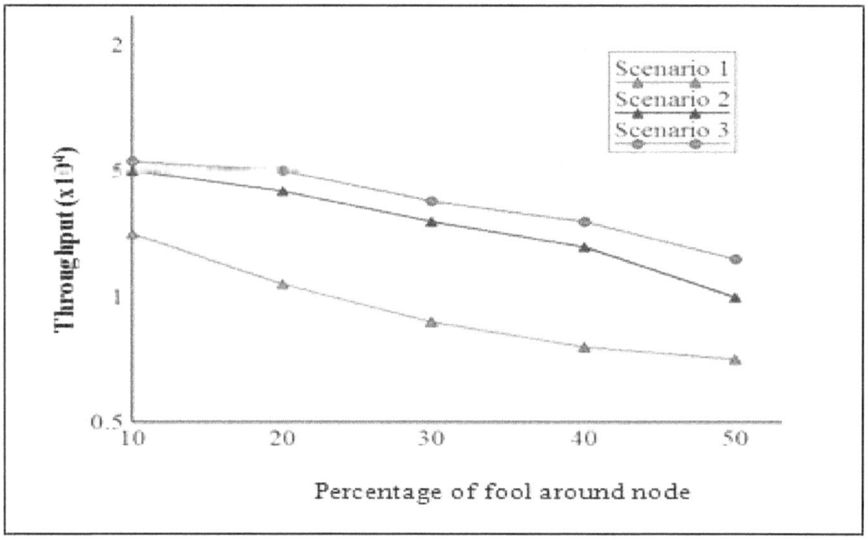


**Figure 6.8 Overall throughput w.r.t various percentage of fool around nodes**

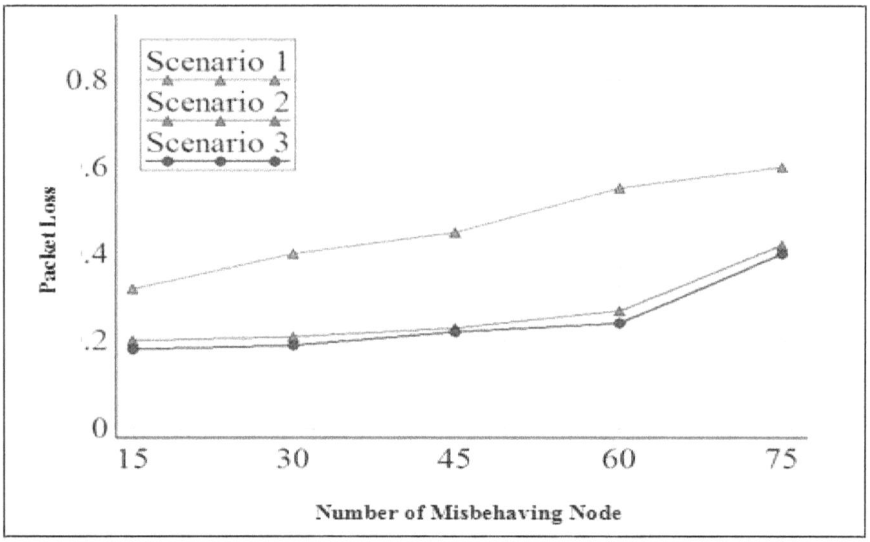


**Figure 6.9 Packet loss w.r.t various percentage of fool around nodes**

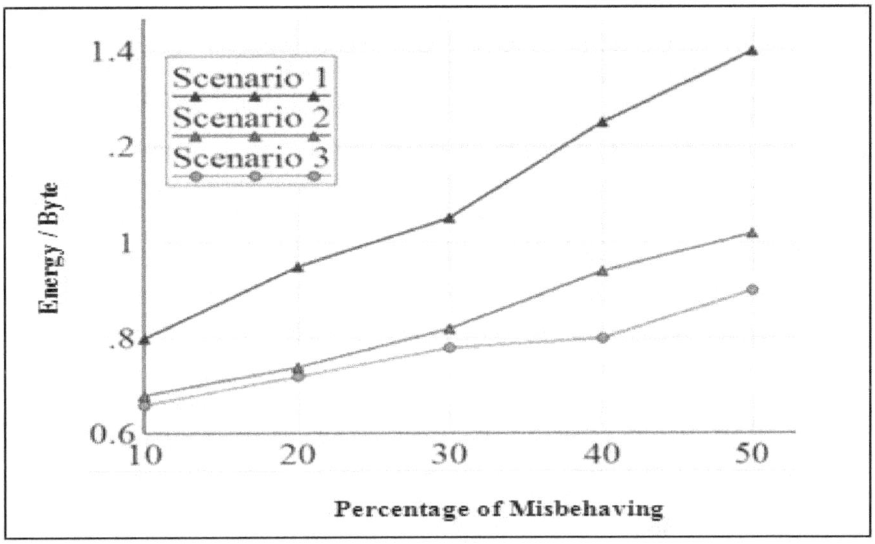


**Figure 6.10 Consumption of energy w.r.t various percentage of fool around nodes**

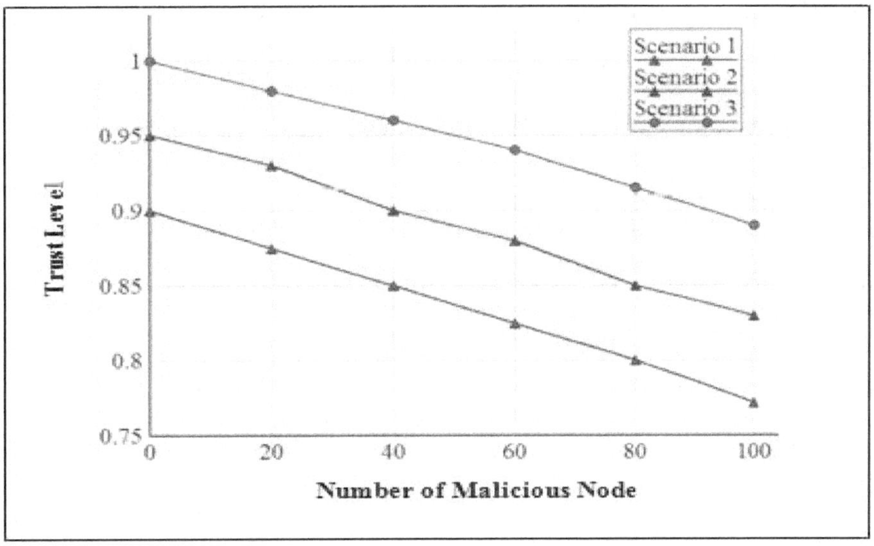


**Figure 6.11 Trust level w.r.t various percentage of fool around nodes**

In the existence of varied proportions of malicious nodes, we can deduce the rate of transmission errors with linear inclinations. It can show that situation 1 has a more significant loss rate, situation 2 has a medium loss rate, and situation 3 has the lowest loss rate. Therefore, we may deduce from the least packet drop ratio that the suggested DPCA approach is efficient even when the fool around node (misbehaving) entity is present inside the wireless network at different percentile levels.

Finally, Figure 6.10 shows that the energy use of nodes in a network exists at varying percentile levels due to the effects of fooling around nodes (misbehaving) nodes. The conclusion is that power consumption increases linearly with the presence of a fool around node (misbehaving) node at various percentage levels in the network. The results show that Situation 1 has a greater energy consumption, Situation 2 has a medium energy usage, and Situation 3 almost has the lowest energy usage. Situation 3 is tested further with situations 1 and 2 using a variety of QoS measurements to determine the level of node trust in a MANET network. Figure 6.11 shows that situation 3 registered a higher level of trust than the other two instances. DPCA Investigation of Total Proportion Change of Parameters.

Overall, the quality parameter evaluations shown in the graph suggest that DPCA reduces delay by 64%. The packet delivery ratio has grown to roughly 82 percent compared to DPCA's 75 percent, and the remaining energy has increased to 89 percent, reducing the node's consumption to a lower value compared with the existing protocol's significant importance. The network's lifetime is extended once the energy usage is lowered regularly. The performance of the DPCA with the Mining algorithm demonstrates the effectiveness of overall metrics.

The proposed Data Path Combinatorial Approach for identifying malicious nodes in MANETs can react to changes in the network by continuously monitoring and analyzing the network traffic. As the nodes in a MANET may be dynamically changing, the approach needs to be able to adapt to these changes to ensure that malicious nodes can be identified in real-time.

To collect the necessary and up-to-date network status, the approach uses data path mining to analyze the traffic generated by the nodes. This approach allows for the identification of patterns and trends in the network traffic, which can be used to identify nodes that are behaving in a suspicious or malicious manner. By continuously analyzing the traffic, the approach can adapt to changes in the network and identify new patterns and trends as they emerge.

However, collecting and analyzing the network traffic can result in increased communication overhead and processing complexity. To minimize the impact on the network, the approach uses combinatorial methods such as frequent itemset generation and approximate inclusion exclusion to optimize the results and reduce the processing complexity. The approach also uses pruning methods to further optimize the results and reduce the communication overhead.

In summary, the proposed Data Path Combinatorial Approach can react to changes in the network by continuously monitoring and analyzing the network traffic. The approach uses data path mining to collect the necessary and up-to-date network status, and combinatorial methods to optimize the results and reduce the processing complexity and communication overhead.

## SUMMARY

This chapter completely deals with the performance analysis of QECC and DEFECT protocol. The performances of various parameters are analyzed such as throughput, packet sent successfully, trusted path finding, error rate and energy consumption. The simulation result shows that the QECC and DEFECT are performed better than the existing protocol. Finally, the proposed approach assuring that the energy efficiency, and throughput are increased to prolong the overall network is secure and safe for transmission of packets.

# CHAPTER 7

# CONCLUSION AND FUTURE WORK

## CONCLUSION

The Mobile Ad hoc Network security is an emerging trend with many applications. The ad hoc network doesn't have any permanent solution for infrastructure-less secure communication. The nodes are deployed randomly in an area with different features to monitor the environment and to collect the data. The collected data are not able to transmit the data packet from source to sink node which need face more problems such change of topology, energy consumption, more error due to attacks, and packet delivery ratio which need to achieve. The MANET works more efficient in the static node but in the mobility is very difficult to do the transmission due in secure of data in dynamic topology and mobility of nodes..

This cryptographic approach is offered as a way to start a robust public-key cryptographic system for securing network connectivity. In recent years, this cryptographic technology has advanced in both the industry and academia fields. When faced with a discrete logarithm problem, ECDSA requires whole exponential time to solve it, whereas RSA and DSA both need sub-exponential time to handle discrete logarithm problems. Furthermore, ECDSA is a technology that allows for lower-key lengths and requires less capacity to provide safe transmission. Compared to RSA and DSA, many variables can be employed more quickly and productively in ECDSA.

Aside from that, the tiny key size, fast calculation, low power consumption, limited storage space, and limited bandwidth are just a few of the main aspects that make ECDSA one of the best and most ideal options for protecting network connectivity. However, because WSNs are limited networks, and ECDSA is best suited for constrained networks, these qualities of ECDSA have made it a good fit for our network. This research work has presented a secure and efficient technique for secure transmission over a wireless network of 100 nodes. The protocol was developed using elliptic curve encryption and examined two forms of communication: interaction between nodes of the same type and interaction between nodes of various kinds.

The primary goal of this study was to develop a secure protocol for sensor nodes that would allow only authorized nodes to connect, lowering the cost of risk and potential risks on the network. We looked at three different parameters to see how well our suggested technique performed. First, we looked at the packet size transferred between the nodes. Second, we looked at the overall number of 'hello' signals sent during the interaction between two nodes of the same type. Finally and not distant, the key creation time for creating paired keys was evaluated as the third variable. It has been determined from the evaluation of this suggested technique that creating paired keys for the network's weaker nodes can help reduce energy usage.

Furthermore, this suggested technique offers all network nodes authenticity, confidentiality, and non-repudiation. However, it has been discovered that network deployment time substantially impacts the formation of keys on nodes. Our suggested technique achieves several practical security aspects in real-world applications where performance and security are key considerations. The QECC's effectiveness is modeled and assessed using a variety of metrics. The resulting findings are compared with the existing AWSC methodology. Compared to QECC, the average trustworthy path observed in QECC is approximately 46 percent higher, implying that a more significant number of nodes will be vulnerable to malicious attacks. In AWSC, massive packet loss occurs due to the fool node; however, in QECC, the secured data packet transferred to the sink node is improved by 68 percent, and packet loss is decreased. The higher the energy efficiency, the lower the mistake rate becomes. Compared to the AWSC, the QECC has a 48 percent lower mistake rate. The nodes can easily share data in the network with pair-wise key generation, which decreases the danger. As the node's energy improves, so does the network's life expectancy. Compared to AWSC, QECC saves up to 60% of the power.

The frequent node sets from MANET data stream are extracted using the Data Path Combinatorial Approximation (DPCA) algorithm in the second developed framework. Nodes that do not engage in the broadcasting of frequent sets are banned and will be checked more closely in the future. To determine the approximate count of common node sets, the approximation inclusion-exclusion technique, skip and completion technique, and group counting approach was used. Instead of continuously examining the routes, the DPCA method employed the basis information. The skip and completion strategy helped to shorten response time. The lexicographic order prefix tree was employed in the group counting approach to representing the frequent node-set. The suggested algorithm's storage was assessed using base data. Consequently, when the minimum support is equivalent to 20%, the DPCA method achieves better results.

We may deduce from the influence of energy usage and node accuracy that node engagement and frequent successful transactions grow;

however, energy usage appears to rise caused by malicious node activities, which exponentially diminishes the trust value. Data overloading can arise when node sets are generated frequently from the data channel. Data overloading management strategies can be adopted in the future for efficient information congestion management, and we can enhance our investigation in numerous areas such as safety, networking life span, bandwidth allocation, and so on, as shown below.

**Security Enhancement:** MANET mining algorithms can be used to identify fool around nodes or various attacks like black-holes, worm-hole assaults, etc. We can get rid of a breakdown of trusted networks by examining and mining frequent node sets in MANET using previous transactions at each node.

**Increased Network Life Span:** In a MANET, saving energy is critical. As a result, homogeneity should be preserved and must maximize energy utilization at each node. Our DPCA approach aids in the detection of active and inactive nodes. The presence of rogue nodes in a network generates superfluous traffic and places additional strain on active nodes, reducing the network's lifespan.

**Load balancing:** It is an essential factor in MANET. By minimizing the number of connections among nodes within the network, engaged nodes will be less burdened, and the system's load will be spread across all active nodes.

## FUTURE WORKS

Based on the proposed Data Path Combinatorial Approach for identifying malicious nodes in a MANET, there are several areas for future work that could be explored, such as:

- Improvement of algorithm efficiency: The proposed approach uses combinatorial methods, which can be computationally intensive. Future work could investigate ways to improve the efficiency of the algorithm, such as by exploring parallel computing methods or optimizing the algorithm's implementation.

- Scalability: The approach should be tested on larger MANET networks to determine its scalability. Future research could focus on developing methods to handle larger networks, such as by partitioning the network and applying the approach to each partition.

- Comparison with cryptographic methods: The proposed approach is non-cryptographic, and future work could compare its performance with cryptographic methods like QECC and ECC to identify their relative strengths and weaknesses in identifying malicious nodes.

- Detection of more complex attacks: The proposed approach is effective at detecting simple malicious behaviors, such as packet dropping and modification. Future work could focus on developing methods to detect more complex attacks, such as collusion attacks, Sybil attacks, and wormhole attacks.

- Implementation and real-world testing: The proposed approach has not been implemented or tested in a real-world scenario. Future work could focus on implementing the approach in a testbed or simulation to evaluate its performance and effectiveness in identifying malicious nodes in a MANET.

- The system, as mentioned earlier, is utilized for safe data transfer verification, session key authentication, privacy, intractability, and resilience to various assaults; our suggested algorithm's secure capability lets it be employed in different real-world situations.

- Research security is a critical duty. In the future, the integration to protect the information will help to increase the network's performance by reducing the number of vulnerable assaults.

- Wireless Sensor Network (WSN): The advantages of our DPCA theory at multiple levels in MANET can be applied to WSNs, allowing us to improve our strategy for WSNs in future studies.

- It will take a long time to recover the failing nodes.

# REFERENCES


1. Abdesslem Layeb 2011, 'A novel quantum inspired cuckoo search for Knapsack problems', International Journal of Bio-Inspired Computation, vol. x, no. x.

2. Aliero, MS, Ghani, I, Qureshi, KN & Rohani, MFA 2020, 'An algorithm for detecting SQL injection vulnerability using black-box testing', Journal of Ambient Intelligence and Humanized Computing. vol. 11, no. 1, pp. 249-266.

3. Ananda Rao, G, Srinivas, Y, Vijaya Sekhar, J & Pavan Kumar, CH 2011, 'Three Party Authentication Key Distributed Protocols Using Implicit and Explicit Quantum Cryptography', Indian Journal of Computer Science and Engineering, vol. 2, no. 2, pp. 143-145.

4. Anju Chahal, Anuj Kumar & Auradha 2014, 'Secure Key Management in Ad-Hoc Network: A Review', International Journal of Advances in Engineering & Technology, vol. 7, no. 3, pp. 1009-1017.

5. ANSI X9.62 1999, 'Public Key Cryptography for the Financial Services Industry: The Elliptic Curve Digital Signature Algorithm (ECDSA)', American National Standards Institute, New York, USA.

6. Aranganathan, A & Suriyakala, CD 2019,'An efficient secure detection and prevention of malevolent nodes with lightweight surprise check scheme using trusted mobile agents in mobile ad-hoc networks', J Ambient Intell Human Comput, vol. 10, pp. 3493-3503.

7. Assche, GV 2006, 'Quantum Cryptography and Secret-Key Distillation', Cambridge Univ. Press.

8. Avanzi, RM 2004, 'Aspects of hyper elliptic curves over large prime fields in software implementations', Cryptographic Hardware and Embedded Systems - CHES, Lecture Notes in Computer. Sci., Springer-Verlag, vol. 3156, pp. 148-162.

9. Bennett, CH & Brassard, G 1983, 'Quantum cryptography and its application to provably secure key expansion, public-key distribution, and coin-tossing', In: IEEE International Symposium on Information Theory (ISIT), p. 91.

10. Bennett, CH & Brassard, G 1984, 'Quantum cryptography: Public key distribution and coin tossing', IEEE International Conference on Computers, Systems, and Signal Processing, pp. 175-179.

11. Bennett, CH & Brassard, G 1987, 'Quantum public key distribution reinvented', Sigact News, vol. 18, no. 4, pp. 51-53.

12. Bennett, CH, Brassard, G & Breidbart, S 1982, 'Quantum cryptography II: How to re-use a one-time pad safely even if P = NP', Unpublished Manuscript.

13. Bennett, CH, Brassard, G & Ekert, AK 1992, 'Quantum cryptography', Sci. Am., vol. 267, no. 4, pp. 50.

14. Bennett, CH, Brassard, G & Mermin, ND 1992, 'Quantum cryptography without bells theorem', Phys. Rev. Lett., vol. 68, pp. 557.

15. Bennett, CH, Brassard, G, Breidbart, S & Wiesner, S 1982, 'Quantum cryptography, or unforgeable subway tokens', In: CRYPTO 1982, Plenum, New York, pp. 267-275.

16. Biehl, I, Meyer, B & Muller, V 2000, 'Differential Fault Attacks on Elliptic Curve Cryptosystems', Proc. of Crypto, LNCS 1880, pp. 131-146.

17. Bing Wu, Jie Wu & Mihaela Cardei 2008, 'A Survey of Key Management in Mobile Ad Hoc Networks', Handbook of Research On Wireless Security, pp. 1-23.

18. Birkhoff, G & von Neumann, J 1936, 'The Logic of Quantum Mechanics', Annals of Mathematics, vol. 37, pp. 823-843.

19. Blaze, M 1993, 'A cryptographic file system for UNIX', Proceedings of the 1st ACM conference on Computer and communications security Fairfax, Virginia, United States ACM Press, pp. 9-16.

20. Brassard, C & Crepeau, C 1990, 'Quantum bit commitment and coin tossing protocols', In: CRYPTO 1990, Lecture Notes in Computer Science, Springer, Berlin, vol. 537, pp. 49-61.

21. Brassard, G & Salvail, L 1994, 'Secret key reconciliation by public discussion', in Advances in Cryptology: EUROCRYPT'93, ser. Lecture Notes in Computer Science, T. Helleseth, Ed., Springer-Verlag, Berlin, Germany, vol. 765, pp.410-423.

22. Brassard, G 2005, 'Brief history of quantum cryptography: A personal perspective', IEEE Information Theory Workshop on Theory and Practice in Information-Theoretic Security, IEEE, New York, pp. 19-23.

23. Brassard, G, Crepeau, C, Jozsa, R & Langlois, D 1993, 'A quantum bit commitment scheme provably unbreakable by both parties', 34th Annual IEEE Symposium on Foundations of Computer Science (FOCS), pp. 362-371.

24. Bruss, D 1998, 'Optimal eavesdropping in quantum cryptography with six states', Phys. Rev. Lett., vol. 81, pp. 3018.

25. Chandra, KR, Sahoo, SK & Behera, SK 2023, 'Quantum Cryptography Based on Elliptic Curve Cryptography for Secure Data Transmission', International Journal of Communication Systems, vol. 36, no. 1, e5041.

26. Chao-Wei Li, Kuen-Fang Jea, Ru-Ping Lin, Ssu-Fan Yen & Chih-Wei Hsu 2012,'Mining frequent patterns from dynamic data streams with data load management'. J. Syst. Softw. vol. 85, no. 6, pp. 1346-1362.

27. Chen, T, Cao, J & Liu, X 2022, 'QSMC: A Quantum Secret Sharing Scheme Based on Minkowski Sum with Elliptic Curve Cryptography', Journal of Ambient Intelligence and Humanized Computing, vol. 13, no. 1, pp. 171-182.

28. Chen, Y, Li, W & Zhang, H 2023, 'Quantum Elliptic Curve Cryptography with Cloud Computing', Journal of Ambient Intelligence and Humanized Computing, vol. 14, no. 1, pp. 195-206.

29. Chiranjibe Jana & Madhumangal Pal 2018, 'Application of Bipolar Intuitionistic Fuzzy Soft Sets in Decision Making Problem', Int. J. Fuzzy Syst. Appl. vol. 7, no. 3, pp. 32-55.

30. Chown, M 2007, 'Quantum Theory Cannot Hurt You: A Guide to the Universe', Faber and Faber.

31. Cui, Y, Li, M & Wang, C 2022, 'Quantum Public Key Cryptography Based on Elliptic Curve Cryptography', Journal of Information Security and Applications, vol. 68, 102973.

32. Dagmar Bruss Gabor ErdeLyi, Tim Meyer, Tobias Riege & JoRgRo 2007, 'Quantum Cryptography: A Survey', ACM Computing Surveys, vol. 39, no. 2, Article 6.

33. Darvish, M 2021, 'Quantum Key Distribution based on Correlated Probabilistic Polarization', IEEE Communications Letters, vol. 25, no. 6, pp. 1866-1869.

34. Deng Zhi-Hong & Lv Sheng-Long 2014, 'Fast mining frequent itemsets using Nodesets. Expert Systems with Applications', vol. 41, pp. 4505-4512.

35. Fei Gao, Su-Juan Qin, Fen-ZhuoGuo & Qiao-Yan Wen 2010, 'Dense-Coding Attack on Three-Party Quantum Key Distribution Protocols', IEEE Journal of Quantum Electronics, vol. X, no. X, pp. 1-6.

36. Feng, T & Chang, Y 2011, 'Combinatorial Constructions for Optimal Two-Dimensional Optical Orthogonal Codes With $\lambda=2$', IEEE Transactions on Information Theory, vol. 57, no. 10, pp. 6796-6819.

37. Gan Gao 2010, 'Cryptanalysis of multiparty quantum secret sharing with collective eavesdropping-check', Journal Optics Communications, vol. 283, no. 14, pp. 2997-3000.

38. Ganesan, R & Vivekanadan, K 2011, 'Comparative analysis of higher genus hyperelliptic curve cryptosystems over finite field $F_P$', ICTACT Journal on Communication Technology, vol. 02, issue 01, pp. 238-240.

39. Gay, S 2006, 'Quantum Programming Languages: Survey and Bibliography', in Mathematical Structures in Computer Science, Cambridge University Press, vol. 16, no. 4.

40. Gomathy, V, Padhy, N & Samanta, D 2020, 'Malicious node detection using heterogeneous cluster based secure routing protocol (HCBS) in wireless adhoc sensor networks', J Ambient Intell Human Comput.

41. Gurmeet Singh Manku & Rajeev Motwani 2002, 'Approximate frequency counts over data streams', In Proceedings of the 28th international conference on Very Large Data Bases (VLDB '02). VLDB Endowment, pp. 346-357.

42. Gurung, S & Chauhan, S 2018, 'A novel approach for mitigating route request flooding attack in MANET', Wireless Netw, vol. 24, pp. 2899-2914.

43. I-Ching Yu, Feng-Li Liny & Ching-Yu Huangz 2008, 'Quantum secret sharing with multilevel mutually (un)biased base', Phys. Rev letters, vol. 78, no. 1, pp. 1-5.

44. Jana, C, Muhiuddin, G & Pal, M 2019, 'Multiple-attribute decision making problems based on SVTNH methods', J Ambient Intell Human Comput.

45. Jana, C, Pal, M & Wang, J 2019, 'Bipolar fuzzy Dombi aggregation operators and its application in multiple-attribute decision-making process', J Ambient Intell Human Comput, vol. 10, pp. 3533-3549.

46. Jana, C, Senapati, T & Pal, M 2020, 'Different types of cubic ideals in BCI-algebras based on fuzzy points', Afr. Mat., vol. 31, pp. 367-381.

47. Jea Kuen-Fang & Li Chao-Wei 2009, 'Discovering frequent itemsets over transactional data streams through an efficient and stable approximate approach', Expert Syst. Appl., vol. 36, pp. 12323-12331.

48. Jeong, YS & Lee, SH 2007, 'Hybrid Key Establishment Protocol Based on ECC for Wireless Sensor Network', International conference on ubiquitous intelligence and computing.

49. Karthikeyan, K, Ramesh, S & Kirubakaran, N 2020, 'Advanced resilient data consigning mechanism for mobile adhoc networks', J Ambient Intell Human Comput.

50. Kessl, R 2016, 'Probabilistic Static Load-Balancing of Parallel Mining of Frequent Sequences', IEEE Transactions on Knowledge and Data Engineering, vol. 28, no. 5, pp. 1299-1311.

51. Khan, MB, Ullah, I & Sohail, A 2021, 'A Novel Quantum Cryptography Approach using Randomized Entangled Qubits', Journal of Ambient Intelligence and Humanized Computing, vol. 12, no. 12, pp. 12363-12376.

52. Koblitz, N 1987, 'Elliptic Curve Cryptosystems', Mathematics of Computation, pp. 203-209.

53. Kuen-Fang Jea, Ming-Yuan Chang & Ke-Chung Lin 2004,'An efficient and flexible algorithm for online mining of large itemsets'. Inf. Process. Lett., vol. 92, no. 6, pp. 311-316.

54. Kuk-Hyun Han & Jong-Hwan Kim 2002, 'Quantum-inspired evolutionary algorithm for a class of combinatorial optimization', IEEE Transactions on Evolutionary Computation, vol. 6, issue 6, pp. 580-593.

55. Kukreja, D, Dhurandher, SK & Reddy, BVR 2018, 'Power aware malicious nodes detection for securing MANETs against packet forwarding misbehavior attack', J Ambient Intell Human Comput, vol. 9, pp. 941-956.

56. Kumar, A & Pais, AR 2019, 'A new combinatorial design based key pre-distribution scheme for wireless sensor networks', J Ambient Intell Human Comput, vol. 10, pp. 2401-2416.

57. Kumar, A & Sharma, A 2022, 'Efficient Quantum Key Distribution Scheme using an Improved Elliptic Curve Cryptography', Proceedings of the 2022 International Conference on Communication, Computing and Networking (ICCCN), pp. 1-6.

58. Kumar, R, Sharma, R & Shukla, A 2022, 'Quantum elliptic curve cryptography: New trends and future prospects', Journal of Ambient Intelligence and Humanized Computing, vol. 13, no. 3, pp. 2955-2972.

59. Kumar, V, Jain, A & Barwal, P 2014, 'Wireless sensor networks: security issues, challenges and solutions', International Journal of Information and Computer Technology, vol. 4, no. 8, pp. 859-868.

60. Li, Y & Wei, Y 2022, 'Quantum Elliptic Curve Cryptography Using Qubits in Nuclear Magnetic Resonance', Journal of Computational and Theoretical Nanoscience, vol. 19, no. 3, pp. 1204-1211.

61. Linial, N & Nisan, N 1990, 'Approximate Inclusion-Exclusion', Combinatorica, vol. 10, pp. 349-365.

62. Liu, CL 1968, 'Introduction to combinatorial mathematics', New York: McGraw-Hill.

63. Liu, J, Wang, K & Fung, BCM 2016, 'Mining High Utility Patterns in One Phase without Generating Candidates', IEEE Transactions on Knowledge and Data Engineering, vol. 28, no. 5, pp. 1245-1257.

64. Lu, J, Hu, Y, Zhang, Y & Xu, J 2023, 'A Secure Quantum Key Distribution Protocol Based on Elliptic Curve Cryptography', IEEE Transactions on Information Forensics and Security, vol. 18, no. 1, pp. 77-88.

65. Majid Safari & Murat Uysal 2009, 'Relay-Assisted Quantum-Key Distribution Over Long Atmospheric Channels', Journal of Light Wave Technology, vol. 27, no. 20, pp. 4508-4515.

66. Makur, D, Singh, H & Kumar, A 2022, 'Quantum Elliptic Curve Cryptography: A Review', International Journal of Quantum Information, vol. 20, no. 5, 2141001.

67. Manikantan, K & Dhanalakshmi, R 2021, 'An Improved Quantum Elliptic Curve Cryptography using Energy Efficient Routing for Mobile Ad-hoc Network', Proceedings of the 2021 5th International Conference on Intelligent Computing and Control Systems (ICCS), pp. 1385-1390.

68. Mark Hillery, Vladimir Buzek & Andre Berthiaume 1999, 'Quantum secret sharing', Physical Review A, vol. 59, no. 3.

69. Mirjalili, SH 2021, 'Secure Communication Protocol using Quantum Elliptic Curve Cryptography with Genetic Algorithm', Journal of Ambient Intelligence and Humanized Computing, vol. 12, no. 9, pp. 10275-10287.

70. Mohamed Elboukhari, Abdelmalek Azizi & Mustafa Azizi 2010, 'Integration of Quantum Cryptography in the TLS Protocol: Reality and Perspectives', MICS'10 International conference, Ensias, Rabat Morocco.

71. Mozaffari-Kermani, MR, Naeini, SM & Soleimani, E 2021, 'Quantum Cryptography Based on Quantum Elliptic Curve Cryptography and its Applications', Journal of Computational and Theoretical Nanoscience, vol. 18, no. 1, pp. 372-378.

72. Muhammad Mubashir Khan & JieXu 2012, 'Quantum Cryptography with Generalized Bases and Dimensions of Photon States', International Journal of Security and Its Applications, vol. 6, no. 1, pp. 49-56.

73. Narayan, AB, Mistry, A & Vyas, H 2023, 'Multi-factor Authentication for Cloud-based IoT Using Quantum Computing', Journal of Cloud Computing, vol. 12, no. 1, p. 23.

74. Nivedita, V & Nandhagopal, N 2020, 'Improving QoS and efficient multi-hop and relay based communication frame work against attacker in MANET', J Ambient Intell Human Comput.

75. NurAtiqah Muhammad & Zuriati Ahmad Zukarnain 2009, 'Implementation of BB84 Quantum Key Distribution Protocol's with Attacks', European Journal of Scientific Research, vol. 32, no. 4, pp. 460-466.

76. Park, SH, Lee, JH & Kim, JH 2021, 'An Efficient Quantum Cryptographic System with ECC and QKD for WSN', Sensors, vol. 21, no. 19, 6417.

77. Qureshi, KN & Abdullah, AH 2014, 'Adaptation of wireless sensor network in industries and their architecture, standards and applications', World Application Science Journal, vol. 30, no. 10, pp. 1218-1223.

78. Qureshi, KN, Abdullah, AH, Bashir, F, Iqbal, S & Awan, KM 2018, 'Cluster-based data dissemination, cluster head formation under sparse, and dense traffic conditions for vehicular ad hoc networks', International Journal of Communication System, vol. 31, no. 8.

79. Qureshi, KN, Bashir, F & Abdullah, AH 2017, 'Provision of security in vehicular ad hoc networks through an intelligent secure routing scheme', In: Paper presented at the 2017 international conference on frontiers of information technology (FIT).

80. Qureshi, KN, Din, S, Jeon, G & Piccialli, F 2020, 'Link quality and energy utilization based preferable next hop selection routing for wireless body area networks', Computer Communication, vol. 149, pp. 382-392.

81. Rahul Aggarwal, Heeren Sharma & Deepak Gupta 2011, 'Analysis of Various Attacks over BB84 Quantum Key Distribution Protocol', International Journal of Computer Applications, vol. 20, no. 8, pp. 28-31.

82. Rajput, M & Ghawte, U 2017, 'Security Challenges in Mobile Ad hoc Networks', International Journal of Computer Application, vol. 168, pp. 24-29.

83. Rakesh Agrawal & Ramakrishnan Srikant 1994, 'Fast Algorithms for Mining Association Rules in Large Databases', In Proceedings of the 20th International Conference on Very Large Data Bases (VLDB '94). Morgan Kaufmann Publishers Inc., San Francisco, CA, USA, pp. 487-499.

84. Ramkumar, B, Dua, S & Pandey, S 2022, 'QELIP: A Post-Quantum Signature Scheme Based on Elliptic Curve Cryptography and Quantum Key Distribution', IEEE Transactions on Quantum Engineering, vol. 4, pp. 1-11.

85. Rashad, MZ, Keshk, AE, El-Dosuky, MA & Kamal, MM 2014, 'Genetic Cuckoo Optimization Algorithm (GCOA)', International Journal of Computer Applications, vol. 90, no. 3, pp. 7-12.

86. Rasheed, M, Adnan, M, Khan, SA & Saleem, S 2022, 'Post-Quantum Secure and Efficient Elliptic Curve Cryptography for MANET', Wireless Personal Communications, vol. 127, no. 1, pp. 685-704.

87. Rashid, MM, Gondal, I & Kamruzzaman, J 2015, 'Share-Frequent Sensor Patterns Mining from Wireless Sensor Network Data', IEEE Transactions on Parallel and Distributed Systems, vol. 26, no. 12, pp. 3471-3484.

88. Rawassizadeh, Reza, Momeni Elaheh Dobbins, Chelsea Gharibshah, Joobin Pazzani & Michael 2016, 'Scalable Daily Human Behavioral Pattern Mining from Multivariate Temporal Data', IEEE Transactions on Knowledge and Data Engineering, vol. 28, pp. 3098-3112.

89. Richard Stern, Nikhil Joshi, Kaijie Wu & Ramesh Karri 2007, 'Register Transfer Level Concurrent Error Detection in Elliptic Curve Crypto Implementations', Proceeding FDTC '07 Proceedings of the Workshop on Fault Diagnosis and Tolerance in Cryptography, IEEE Computer Society Washington, DC, USA, pp.112-119.

90. Rishi Dutt Sharma 2011, 'Quantum Cryptography: A new approach to information security', International Journal of Power System Operation and Energy Management (IJPSOEM), vol. 1, no. 1, pp. 11-13.

91. Rosheen Qazi, Kashif Naseer Qureshi, Faisal Bashir, Najam Ul Islam & Saleem Iqbal Arsalan Arshad, 2019, 'Security protocol using elliptic curve cryptography algorithm for wireless sensor networks', Journal of Ambient Intelligence and Humanized Computing, vol. 11, no. 5.

92. Saha, S, Roy, B & Ghosh, A 2022, 'Quantum Elliptic Curve Cryptography for Secure and Efficient Communication in IoT Networks', Journal of Ambient Intelligence and Humanized Computing, vol. 13, no. 6, pp. 7587-7602.

93. Sathi Reddy, K & Raja Kumar Medapati 2011, 'Three Party Quantum Authenticated Key Distribution Protocol Using Superposition States', Int. J. Comp. Tech. Appl., vol. 2, no. 5, pp. 1589-1594.

94. Seo, SC, Kim, HC & Ramakrishna, R 2006, 'A New Security Protocol Based On Elliptic Curve Cryptosystems For Securing Wireless Sensor Networks', The international conference on embedded and ubiquitous computing.

95. Singh, R, Sharma, M & Pandey, AK 2022, 'Quantum Enhanced Digital Signatures: A Review', Journal of Quantum Computing, vol. 3, no. 1, pp. 15-28.

96. Sumalatha, MS & Nandalal, V 2020, 'An intelligent cross layer security based fuzzy trust calculation mechanism (CLS-FTCM) for securing wireless sensor network (WSN)', J Ambient Intell Human Comput.

97. Tseng, VS, Wu, C, Fournier-Viger, P & Yu, PS 2016, 'Efficient Algorithms for Mining Top-K High Utility Itemsets', IEEE Transactions on Knowledge and Data Engineering, vol. 28, no. 1, pp. 54-67.

98. Ubaidullah Rajput, Fizza Abbas & Heekuck Oh 2016, 'A Hierarchical Privacy Preserving Pseudonymous Authentication Protocol for VANET', IEEE Access, vol. 4, pp. 7770-7784.

99. Veronica Fernandez, Robert J Collins, Karen J Gordon, Paul D Townsend & Gerald S Buller 2007, 'Passive Optical Network Approach to Giga Hertz-Clocked Multiuser Quantum Key Distribution', IEEE Journal of Quantum Electronics, vol. 43, no. 2, pp. 1-9.

100. Wang Jian, Zhang Quan & Tang Chao-Jing 2007, 'Multiparty Quantum Secret Sharing of Secure Direct Communication Using Teleportation'.

101. Wegman, MN & Carter, JL 1979, 'Universal classes of hash functions', J. Comput. Syst. Sci., vol. 18, pp. 143-154.

102. Wei, Z, Li, J, Wang, X & Gao, CZ 2019, 'A Lightweight Privacy-Preserving Protocol for VANET's Based on Secure Outsourcing Computing', IEEE Access, vol. 7, pp. 62785-62793.

103. Wu, L & Wu, X 2021, 'Enhanced Quantum Cryptography Based on Elliptic Curve Cryptography and Chaotic Maps', Journal of Systems Science and Complexity, vol. 34, no. 4, pp. 1341-1359.

104. Yan Zhang, Fan Zhang, Zheming Jin & Jason D Bakos 2013, 'An FPGA-Based Accelerator for Frequent Itemset Mining. ACM Trans', Reconfigurable Technol. Syst., vol. 6, no. 1, p. 17.

105. Yan-Bing Li, Tian-Yin Wang, Hui-Yan Chen, Meng-Dong Li & Ya-Tao Yang 2013, 'Fault-Tolerate Quantum Private Comparison Based on GHZ States and ECC', International Journal of Theoretical Physics, vol. 52, issue 8, pp. 2818-2825.

106. Yao-Hsin Chou, Chia-Hui Chiu & Yi-Jyuan Yang 2011, 'Quantum-Inspired Tabu Search Algorithm for Solving 0/1 Knapsack Problems', ACM transactions, IEEE transactions on evolutionary computation, vol.6, no.6, pp. 580-593.

107. Yao-Hsin Chou, Yi-Jyuan Yang & Chia-Hui Chiu 2011, 'Systems, Man and Cybernetics (SMC)', IEEE International Conference, pp. 1364-1369.

108. Yeh, HL, Chen, TH, Liu, PC, Kim, TH & Wei, HW 2011, 'A secured authentication protocol for wireless sensor networks using elliptic curves cryptography', Journal of Sensors, MDPI, vol. 11, no. 5, pp. 4767-4779.

109. Yong Yu, Bo Yang & Ying Sun 2007, 'A Provably Secure ID-Based Mediated Signcryption Scheme', Eighth ACIS International Conference on Software Engineering, Artificial Intelligence, Networking, and Parallel/Distributed Computing, IEEE Computer Society, pp. 647-652.

110. Yun Jin Choi & Young-Jai Park 2011, 'Multiparty Quantum Secret Sharing Using a Single Not-so-weak Qubit', Journal of the Korean Physical Society, vol. 59, no. 4, pp. 2658-2663.

111. Zakaria Laboudi & Salim Chikhi 2012, 'Comparison of Genetic Algorithm and Quantum Genetic Algorithm', The International Arab Journal of Information Technology, vol. 9, no. 3.

112. Zhang Xing Lan 2009, 'One-way quantum identity authentication based on public key', Chinese Science Bulletin, vol. 54, no. 12, pp. 2018-2021.

113. Zhang, F, Liu, M & Gui, F 2015, 'A distributed frequent itemset mining algorithm using Spark for Big Data analytics', Cluster Comput., vol. 18, pp. 1493-1501.

114. Zhang, J, Jiang, L & Zhang, S 2022, 'A Quantum-Elliptic Curve Cryptography-Based Signcryption Scheme for the Internet of Things', Wireless Personal Communications, vol. 123, no. 1, pp. 351-372.

115. Zhang, S, Du, Z & Wang, JTL 2015, 'New Techniques for Mining Frequent Patterns in Unordered Trees', IEEE Transactions on Cybernetics, vol. 45, no. 6, pp. 1113-1125.

116. Zhang, X, Li, Y, Li, X, Li, Y & Li, C 2022, 'A Quantum Key Distribution Scheme Using Shor's Algorithm for Elliptic Curve Cryptography', IEEE Access, vol. 10, pp. 177751-177759.

117. Zhiguo Qu, Keeney, J, Robitzsch, S, Zaman, F & Xiaojun Wang 2016, 'Multilevel pattern mining architecture for automatic network monitoring in heterogeneous wireless communication networks', China Communications, vol. 13, no. 7, pp. 108-116.

118. Zhu Zhen-Chao, Zhang Yu-Qing & Fu An-Min 2011, 'Efficient quantum secret sharing scheme with two-particle entangled states', Chin. Phys. B, vol. 20, no. 4.

# LIST OF PUBLICATIONS

**International Journal**

1. **Sudharson, K** & Arun, S 2022, 'Security Protocol Function Using Quantum Elliptic Curve Cryptography Algorithm', Intelligent Automation & Soft Computing, vol. 34, no. 3, pp. 1769-1784, **Impact Factor : 1.647**.

www.ingramcontent.com/pod-product-compliance
Lightning Source LLC
LaVergne TN
LVHW082342200926
848481LV00012B/3421
* 9 7 9 8 2 3 3 0 5 9 5 7 5 *